Department of M...

MW00685555

Maple—Calculus Manual
for Mathematics 240 and 241
THIRD EDITION

JONES AND BARTLETT PUBLISHERS

Sudbury, Massachusetts

BOSTON   TORONTO   LONDON   SINGAPORE

World Headquarters
Jones and Bartlett Publishers
40 Tall Pine Drive
Sudbury, MA 01776
978-443-5000
info@jbpub.com
www.jbpub.com

Jones and Bartlett Publishers Canada
6339 Ormindale Way
Mississauga, Ontario L5V 1J2
Canada

Jones and Bartlett Publishers International
Barb House, Barb Mews
London W6 7PA
United Kingdom

Jones and Bartlett's books and products are available through most bookstores and online booksellers. To contact Jones and Bartlett Publishers directly, call 800-832-0034, fax 978-443-8000, or visit our website www.jbpub.com.

Substantial discounts on bulk quantities of Jones and Bartlett's publications are available to corporations, professional associations, and other qualified organizations. For details and specific discount information, contact the special sales department at Jones and Bartlett via the above contact information or send an email to specialsales@jbpub.com.

Copyright © 2009 by the University of Pennsylvania Department of Mathematics and Jones and Bartlett Publishers, LLC

All rights reserved. No part of the material protected by this copyright may be reproduced or utilized in any form, electronic or mechanical, including photocopying, recording, or by any information storage and retrieval system, without written permission from the copyright owner.

Cover Image: © Jos Leys
Printing and Binding: Courier Stoughton
Cover Printing: Courier Stoughton

ISBN-13: 978-0-7637-6673-3

6048
Printed in the United States of America
12 11 10 09 08   10 9 8 7 6 5 4 3 2 1

How to use this book

This book contains valuable information about the course you are taking (and possibly about the next course you will take), and about Maple and how to find it and how to use it. The book also contains many calculus problems that you will be assigned -- some are to be done using Maple, and others are to be worked out by hand. The latter include problems from past final exams in our courses -- they will give you an idea of the level of difficulty you can expect on your exams.

Specifically, in this book you will find:

1. **General information** about how calculus courses are organized at Penn, and ways you can get assistance with math -- these range from using your instructors' office hours to taking advantage of help sessions in the residence halls.

2. **Information about where to find Maple** in computer labs on campus, and about electronic means of getting help with calculus and Maple.

3. **Maple Tutorial Information**--everyone is encouraged to work through the Maple Tutorial, Quick Start, available in several places including the Math Department web site and the Maple for students web site at http://www.maplesoft.com/support/training/quickstart.aspx. There will be Maple based assignments and, at the discretion of your professor, some exams may contain Maple-specific questions.

4. **A fairly extensive "Maple manual"** -- which explains some general principles for using Maple, Maple syntax and a little bit about Maple programming. The rest of the manual part is organized around Maple commands. We have made an attempt to explain what many of Maple's sometimes-mysterious error messages mean, and what to do when you encounter them. The last part of this manual includes a chapter by chapter overview of the use of Maple to solve problems in the Calculus.

5. **Solutions in Maple to selected problems** from the textbook --- These problems are chosen from among your course's "core problems"; they provide an idea of how to solve Calculus problems in Maple. Current versions of this material can be found on the Math. Dept. web site

6. **Sample final exams for your course** --- Some problems from these exams will probably be assigned by your instructor, in addition to problems from the text. More exams are posted on the Math. Dept. web site along with some answer keys.

It is advisable to read through the introductory Maple sections of this book before you have your first Maple session. Before you attempt your first Maple assignment, it would be a good idea to read the sections of the manual on "Basic stuff", "syntax", "solve", and "plot". Before each assignment, you should look through the section on whatever special commands will be used in that assignment.

Although there is a great deal of material in this book, we are always updating it, adding to it, and correcting mistakes when we find them. You can find such additional information on the Math Department's calculus web pages, which are linked from the site

http://www.math.upenn.edu/ugrad/Undergrad.html

PLEASE GIVE US FEEDBACK ABOUT THIS BOOK! We have tried to anticipate many of the questions and problems you will have, but we are sure that we've missed some. If you encounter a problem that is not covered anywhere in this book, or have other suggestions for improving it, please let us know in the Math Department so that we can improve the book for future students.

INFORMATION FOR STUDENTS WHO ARE TAKING

Calculus at Penn

*L*earning calculus has become a central skill in many scientific and professional careers, perhaps the most important skill. Whether calculus proves to be a barrier or a gateway for you depends on how well you learn it. We want you to do as well as you possibly can. It is for this reason that so much structure is provided:

Lecture and Recitations, Office Hours, Homework, Newsgroups and the WWW, Residence-Based Support, The Math & Maple Centers, Review Sessions

There are also the Tutoring and Learning Resources offered by Academic Support Programs, which provides tutoring and reviews. The purpose of this document is to explain what is available.

Lectures and Recitations: Three of your four class hours each week are spent in lecture, where the professor explains the concepts and methods of calculus. At lecture, you should try to get a sense of what is the most important for you to fully understand so that you can study efficiently. Your recitation hour will have a Teaching Assistant (TA) and a smaller group of students. In recitation, attention will focus on the solution of specific calculus problems and kinds of problems. To get the most out of recitation, it is crucial that you have made a serious attempt at the assigned homework in advance. As with any skill, learning the Calculus requires practice in the form of study of the basic theorems, formulas and such plus doing LOTS of problems. Your TA will try to focus on the areas where students are having difficulty; this is clearly impossible if you do not attempt the assignment ahead of time. Please ask questions when you do not follow a problem or demonstration—we can't answer questions you don't ask. Blank stares let us know you don't understand something, but not what it is that is causing difficulty. It is to your advantage to participate actively.

Office Hours: Your professor and TA have office hours that you can attend for additional, more individualized help. If you need such assistance, it is wise not to wait until the week before an exam to go to office hours for the first time, since that is when the professor and TA will be swamped with students.

Homework: Most of your work in calculus will be spent on homework assignments. This can be more time consuming than many other courses. The average student should spend at least 10 hours per week outside of class to master calculus well. This includes time for reading text, solving assigned homework problems (the minimum work required…you should attempt as many problems as you can), working on computer assignments and discussing the harder problems with your study group. Many students will need more than 10 hours per week of practice.

Newsgroups and the WWW: Each calculus course (Math 240 and 241) has a newsgroup. This is an "electronic bulletin board" where you can post questions about either the basic calculus or computer aspects of the course. The questions can be answered either by TAs, who will check the newsgroup regularly, by the professors or by other students. Information about access to the newsgroups is available on the web page of each course.

It is also possible to access the newsgroups by logging into your email account and use a newsreader such as "rn" or "tin". The names of the groups are upenn.math.math 240 and upenn.math.math241. Graduate students will be online several nights each week to answer questions posted to the newsgroups. Some professors also check the newsgroups regularly and provide replies to questions.

The Math Department Web page is another good source of information about math. It can be found at: http://www.math.upenn.edu. This site contains information about the math program at Penn. You should also become familiar with your calculus section's home page. From the Math Department page, select the "Undergraduate Program" link and then scroll down to your course's page. From the course homepage, you can proceed to your instructor's page and your TA's page. More detailed information about how your specific class will be using its home page will be announced in lecture and/or recitation.

Residence-Based Support: Most First-Year College House (and some of the other College Houses) on campus has a Math Advisor. This is an undergraduate who is qualified to assist calculus students with math and Maple. The Math Advisor in each house will announce hours when he or she is available to the residents of the house. Although these programs are primarily residence-based, they are open to all calculus students. In addition, any calculus student who lives off-campus or in a residence without a Math Advisor can choose to affiliate with the Math Advisor of a particular house.

There is a Math and Maple Help web page, which is linked from the Undergraduate Math home page. At this site, you can find a list of the Math Advisors, along with a schedule of the programs they organize and other information about residence-based math and Maple help.

The Math & Maple Centers: The Math Center and the Maple Center are places to go for individual help or to work on homework. The Centers are staffed by graduate mathematics students, and their location rotates among the residence halls on campus. We emphasize that the centers are open to ALL calculus students no matter where they live (but remember to bring your Penn ID to be admitted to the residence hall).

Math and Maple Center hours are from 6:30PM to 9:30PM Monday through Thursday. Locations will be announced in class and posted on the web early each semester. A list is also available from the Math Office in Rittenhouse Laboratory, room 4W1.

What if I have serious D-I-F-F-I-C-U-L-T-I-E-S??

The methods outlined so far are intended for students whose difficulties are more or less manageable. However, if your difficulties are more serious, what should you do? The most important thing is to **Get Advice**. There are a number of options, the best of which is to consult your professor and TA. It is very important that you are directed to the most appropriate one for your situation. You should also consider talking to your academic advisor and making use of the help available through Office of Learning Resources, [Weingarten Learning Resources Center 3702 Spruce Street, Stouffer Commons Suite 300, 215-573-9235].

Getting Advice:
You can come to see the Undergraduate Chairman of the Math Department (Prof. Powers) or the Associate Undergraduate Chairman (Prof. Crotty). You can contact the Math Department office (215-898-8178) DRL 4W1 for their hours and locations. You may also contact them by email, at UGradChair@math.upenn.edu.

Getting Your Act Together:
Successful students do a number of things that greatly increase the effectiveness of the time they spend studying. They tend to use study groups. They take advantage of the various means of help, particularly residential math help, and the Math and Maple Centers. Unsuccessful students are seldom able to organize their work satisfactorily and often misjudge their situation until it is almost too late. If you find yourself getting into these difficulties, you will need to do some reorganizing. A good way to start is by finding out about the math help available in your residence or in other places on campus. Another source of help is the Penn Tutoring and Learning Resource Center, located in Suite 110 of Harnwell House.

Getting a Tutor:
There are two options for getting a tutor:

1. If you feel that your problem is not just math and that more general counseling is in order, you should go for an interview at the Tutoring Center in Suite 110 of Harwell House (High Rise East). If you qualify for aid then you will receive financial assistance in getting a tutor. The Penn Learning Resource Center is also a good source of help for general academic difficulties.
2. The Mathematics Department maintains a list of recommended private tutors. For students with special needs, we also have a small amount of money to help in making these tutors available. See the Undergraduate Secretary or the Math Web for the list of tutors, and see Undergraduate Chair if you have a special need.

Changing Calculus Courses:
The Math Department usually permits students who are enrolled in a Calculus class to drop the one they are in and add the previous course in the same sequence until the end of the drop period. This is several weeks after the end of the add period, but it is still permitted. In the way, students who find themselves with "too much advanced placement credit" can drop back into the previous course without losing a semester.

Dropping Mathematics This Term:
This is the **last resort**. Before the end of the drop period, any student may drop any course for any reason, and no indication appears on the transcript. For five weeks after this drop date, a student may withdraw, provided that permission is obtained from an Assistant Dean. A grade of W will appear on the transcript. Thereafter, withdrawal must be applied for via petition and is granted only for special reasons. Part of the petition must be filled out by your professor. You can get a petition from your school office.

COMPUTERS and MAPLE

Important information for students who are taking Calculus

All students in Math 240 and 241 are using *Maple*, a powerful mathematical software package that is capable of doing symbolic, numerical and graphical computations. A copy of the latest version of Maple is bundled with the text for the Math 240-241 Calculus sequence. This software will be used in classroom demonstrations, and you may be required to use it for some of your homework assignments throughout the semester.

Since it is likely that Maple is not completely familiar to you, there is substantial support available to help you learn and use Maple effectively. Here are some answers to some basic questions you may have about Maple and some information about the various sources of Maple help that you can take advantage of.

Whither Maple? We are using **Maple 12**. There are two ways for students to get access to Maple:

1. If you own your own computer, then you can probably run Maple on it. Maple is available at the bookstore for Macintosh, Windows, and Linux computers and a copy is bundled with the course textbook. Be sure to check the system requirements on the package to verify that your computer can run the software.
2. Maple has been installed in most of the computer labs at Penn, including those in residence halls and in academic buildings. In each location, there are Macintosh and/or Windows PCs, where Maple should be found either the Applications folder or the Start Menu, respectively. When you visit a campus lab, it is a good idea to bring a floppy disk or writable CD to save your work. Maple 12 has the ability to email a copy of the current worksheet to anyone you wish—handy for sending yourself a copy if you can't save your work to a floppy or CD or for submitting your work to your TA or professor electronically. Your professor or TA will tell you if electronic submissions are acceptable.

Maple Documentation – It is crucial that everyone have some documentation and references for the use of Maple. Information about the commands we will be using for calculus at Penn is contained in this book. *Use it!!* Browse the manual and refer to it when you have specific questions for doing assignments. Also look at the solved problems for examples of how Maple can be used in situations specific to the part of calculus you are currently studying. The documentation, especially the Maple Help system (available from the Help menu) that comes with the software also provides useful information for using Maple to perform a wide variety of mathematical tasks. Other books about Maple are available at the Penn Bookstore and the usual online bookstores such as bn.com (Barns and Noble) or Amazon.com .

Maple Tutorials – Tutorials and other support materials are available on the Maplesoft corporate web site (www.maplesoft.com). There are a number of tutorials as well as worksheets covering the use of Maple in most of the topics in these courses (see: http://www.maplesoft.com/students/index.aspx and follow the links there).

Maple Help – Several sources of Maple help are available to you during the semester. First, you should go to your professor and TA. They can help you with basic questions during their office hours. However, if you need help outside of those hours, there are Math Advisors and the Maple Center available to help you. See the Calculus General Information section (pp. 3-5 of this manual), and the undergraduate Math web page http://www.math.upenn.edu/ugrad/Undergrad.html

for further information about these programs and other help that is available.

It is important to realize that very little time, if any, will be spent in class discussing Maple syntax. You must learn this from the examples done in class and by reading and experimenting on your own. If you are having trouble doing this on your own, then use the available resources such as your Math Advisor and the Maple Center.

Work Habits -- There are more than 1500 students taking calculus with Maple every semester. Therefore, it is crucial that you develop some good work habits and take precautions so that you do not waste your time or other people's time. We try to schedule computer assignments so that not all classes have assignments due at the same time. But do not leave computer work until the last minute. Inevitably, there will be problems with printers or busy machines or just plain hard math problems and the sometimes confusing Maple syntax. Be sure to begin your work in a timely manner, and work steadily until all assignments are completed. In general, common sense and courtesy will go a long way towards alleviating logistical problems that inevitably arise.

Be sure to save your work on floppy disks or by uploading it to your computer account over the network (Maple 10 includes a "send" command in the file menu which allows you to email a copy of your worksheet to yourself). It is a good idea to begin a separate file for each problem in a long assignment rather than saving your work in one long file. This makes it easier to make small changes, and it saves paper since you don't have to print everything again once you edit.

Lab Locations--A Campus Labs List is posted on the Web, including information on the number and type of computers in each lab, with lab hours and telephone numbers. For general information about using Public Access Computer Labs, see www.upenn.edu/computing/view/labs/.

Here is a list of labs where Maple is accessible:

College House Computing Labs

> **Hamilton Village Area:**
>> DuBois College House (Room 131)
>> Hamilton College House (1st Floor, front)
>> Harrison College House (1st Floor, front)
>> Harnwell College House (Room 207)
>> International Programs (Harnwell, Room 1901)
>> Stouffer College House (Mayer Hall, Study Lounge)
>> Gregory College House (Class of '25, Rooms 13 and 14, basement)
>> Gregory College House (Van Pelt Manor, Room 123)

> **Quad Area:**
>> Fisher Hassenfeld College House (Memorial Tower, first floor)
>> Spruce College House (Room 105, Ashurst)
>> Stouffer College House (Room 171F)
>> Ware College House (McClelland Hall, rear)

> **North Campus Area:**
>> King's Court/English College House (First floor)
>> Sansom Tower East (Basement)
>> Hill College House (First floor)

Other Locations
> Class of 1937 Computer Lab (Van Pelt-Dietrich Library Center, 3420 Walnut St)
> Long Island Friends of Penn Computer Area (Van Pelt-Dietrich Library Center)
> Medical School Microcomputer Center (Ground floor, Biomedical Library, Johnson Pavilion, 36th St. and Hamilton Walk)
> MMETS Macintosh and PC Computer Classrooms (Basement, Rittenhouse Laboratory, 33rd and Walnut Sts.)
> Rosengarten Computer Lab (Van Pelt-Dietrich Library Center)
> School of Nursing Student Computer Lab (Room 210 Nursing Education Building, 420 Guardian Drive)
> Towne PC Lab (Room M62, Towne Building, 220 S 33rd Street)
> Towne Lower Level PC Lab (Basement, Room 144, Towne Building)
> Undergraduate Data Analysis Lab (Rooms 104, 108-9 McNeil Building, 3718 Locust Walk)

These lists were accurate at the time this manual was prepared, but you are advised to check the links mentioned above for the latest lists.

Problems?
If there are any problems with Maple installations, contact your Residential Information
Technology Advisor or the Computer Resource Center.

Mathematics 240–Syllabus and Core Problems

Mathematics 241–Syllabus and Core Problems

Current versions of the syllabi and core problem lists for these and other Calculus courses can be found on the Math Department's web site at:

http://www.math.upenn.edu/ugrad/Undergrad.html

Select your course from the links at the right side of the page. These pages contain lists of the current semester's classes, instructors and TAs, course syllabi, old final exams and other useful information including links to additional Maple materials including an online version of this manual.

Important getting-started information

In this section, we review some fundamental but crucial things about Maple sessions, saving your work, and how to avoid those mysterious things that seem to happen the night before the assignment is due.

One thing to remember is that a good source of information about how to use Maple is the Maple Learning Guide (available from Maplesoft) -- especially the material at the beginning.

Maple sessions

A Maple session is the set of commands you type in, responses Maple gives, and the values or expressions that are assigned to variables, in the order they are typed in. You start a new session every time you quit and restart Maple. You can also start a new session without quitting by entering the command restart;

Distinct from the Maple session is your worksheet, which is the set of typed commands and responses, along with text and graphics that you insert, which you see on the screen. The worksheet is what gets saved, and what gets printed out. The values of variables and loaded packages ("with"s) are **not** saved in the worksheet!

When you reload a saved worksheet, Maple doesn't remember the variables you assigned or the packages you loaded (even though all that information is in the worksheet). To get back to where you were, simply go to the Edit menu, choose *Execute* and then choose *worksheet* from the popup menu that appears. The entire worksheet will be executed again in the order that the statements appear in the worksheet. This is often te source of (very) hard to trace problems if you moved up and down the worksheet, reexecuting statements or changing values of variables, so it is best to work in sequence from top to bottom, retyping a statement (or cutting and pasting) rather than reexecuting a statement then moving elsewhere in the worksheet.

During a Maple session, you can refer to the output of your last (chronological) command with the percent sign %:

> x:=34/13;

$$x := \frac{34}{13}$$

> evalf(%);

$$2.615384615$$

Saving Worksheets

The first time you save your worksheet, or any time you want to change its name, use "Save As..." from the File menu. You will notice that the default filename, before you type anything in, is "*.mw" or the filename field may be completely blank depending on the options you have set in the "Preferences" dialog. It is crucial that you always save files with a name ending in ".mw", like "prob1.mw". If the ".mw" is left off, Maple will put it in for you. Later, you can save changes to the worksheet using "Save" from the File menu. Maple 10 also has a (sometime annoying) "AutoSave" feature which will save a backup of the current state of your worksheet evert few minutes (the usual default is every 3 minutes, but since *autosaves* can essentially bring a session to a halt, you may want to set a longer interval (say 10 minutes or so) or disable *autosaves* entirely (although this is not recommended as Maple has been known to crash.

To get back to an old worksheet, start Maple by clicking on the Maple icon, then choose "Open.." (or "Open Recent" if it is something you worked on recently) from the File menu or simply double-click on the file you wish to work on. To start a new worksheet and session, choose "New" from the File menu.

"Maple doesn't seem to work..."

Sometimes, it seems like Maple is not accepting your commands, or at least is not executing them. There are several things we know of that can cause this:

1. *Don't forget the semicolon* ... if you type 2+3 then enter, Maple will warn you that your statement was missing its semicolon and recent versions (Maple 9, 9.5 and 10) will try to insert a semi-colon (sometime in the wrong spot, unfortunately), or you can go back at put in the semicolon:
> 2+3
Warning, incomplete statement or missing semicolon
>2+3;
$$5$$

2. *Syntax snafus* -- If you are using "for" statements to make lists, or some other kind of programming construction, sometimes you may begin a set of statements (e.g., with a "do" statement) and forget to end it. The simplest, most direct way to get out of this is to type something that you know will cause a syntax error, so Maple will clear its memory and let you start a new statement. The phrase:

> ;;;od;;
Syntax error, reserved word `od` unexpected

almost always works.

3. *Find that library!* -- Some of Maple's specialized commands (for instance, for linear algebra, fancy plotting, statistics, etc) are stored in libraries, and you must tell Maple explicitly to bring

these commands into to the memory by using a "with" statement. This is described in the section of this book concerning Maple syntax. If Maple is just parroting your commands, it is likely that you have forgotten to load the appropriate library.

4. *We are using Maple 10* -- when the Maple screen comes up at the beginning of your session, it should say Maple 10. If it doesn't you may have an outdated version of Maple on your machine (there are a few floating around). If you discover lab machines with old versions, let us know so we can remedy the situation!

Using Maple Help

There are two kinds of help available on-line in Maple. The first is useful if you know the name of the command you need to use, but have forgotten details of its syntax etc.. The way to use this is to type ?commandname at the Maple prompt. For example, to get information on Maple's "tubeplot" command we would type:

> ?tubeplot

A window will open with information about the tubeplot command. The most useful information in the window will be the examples at the bottom.

The other way to find help about aspects of Maple is to use the "Help Browser". This is found in "Quick Help" or "Manuals, Dictionary and more…" under the "Help" menu.

The help screen for any given Maple command contains more information than most people could possibly want about the command, often expressed in a somewhat overly technical manner. However, at the end of almost all of the help screens are indispensable sets of examples of the uses of the command. These examples can be copied (you will find a "Copy Examples" command in the Edit menu when a help page is active), pasted into your worksheet and executed, so you can see what the command does. This is a good way to learn about new commands.

Basic stuff -- assignments, arithmetic and functions

Most of the time, you will be using Maple as a kind of super-calculator. It is possible to write programs in Maple -- we will do this very occasionally, but usually you will be typing in Maple statements expecting a (more-or-less) immediate response. The most basic thing to remember about Maple statements is that they all end either with a semi-colon (; -the usual way to end them) or a colon (: -you will use this occasionally when you don't want to see Maple's output).Note that recent versions of Maple, including Maple 12 don't require the semicolon (or colon) if there is only one statement on a line, but the semicolon is required between commands if you want to type two or more statements on a single line.

The simplest Maple statements involve arithmetic on constants:

```
>  restart: #clears the computer's memory and returns Maple to its
   initial state; removes ALL stored values
>  3+4;
```
$$7 \tag{1}$$

You type in your statement at the > prompt, press "Enter" and then Maple responds with the answer. Note that Maple 12 assigns a number, (1) in the line above, to each output. this number can be used as a shorthand reference to that line--see the examples in later sections of this manual

Other kinds of statements are **assignment** statements, Maple **commands** (for plotting, solving, etc..), **library management** statements (the "with" command for loading special programs into the computer memory), and a few other assorted special statements.

ASSIGNMENT STATEMENTS

These are the most basic and widely used Maple statements. They allow you to give names to expressions you want the computer to remember for later use. Assignment statements **always** have the "colon-equals" format:

> name   :=   expression

The thing on the left side of the := in an assignment must be a **name** -- i.e., a sequence of letters and digits that begins with a letter. Certain names must be avoided (because Maple is already using them) -- a partial list of these is at the end of this section. Note that if you wish to add a comment to a command, ues the number symbol. #, and any following text is ignored (see the **restart:** line above for example)

Unlike algebra, where variables usually stand for numbers and their names are only one letter long, in Maple names can stand for many different kinds of things (for example, it is possible to give a name to an entire equation or a graph -- see the section on the `solve` and `display` commands for more information) and can be quite descriptive. For example, in a basic derivative problem concerning position, velocity and acceleration, it is permissible to use the names "position", "velocity", "acceleration" and "time". A typical statement in such a context might be

```
> position:=34-5*time-16*time^2; # the carat, ^, is Maple's
  exponentiation operator...
```

$$position := 34 - 5\ time - 16\ time^2 \tag{2}$$

```
> velocity := diff(position, time);
```

$$velocity := -5 - 32\ time \tag{3}$$

which means that velocity is the derivative of position with respect to time (`diff` is the name of one of Maple's commands for taking derivatives).

ASSIGNMENTS, BASIC ARITHMETIC and FUNCTIONS:

Let's start with a few simple assignments:
```
> a:=3; b:=5; c:=32/21;
```

$$a := 3$$

$$b := 5$$

$$c := \frac{32}{21} \tag{4}$$

Notice that you can put more than one Maple statement on a line of input. This kind of simple assignment statement is a case where you might want to use a colon instead of a semicolon -- using a semicolon tells Maple to "parrot" your assignment back to you, but a colon would suppress the output:
```
> a:=3: b:=5: c:=32/21: #note the lack of ooutput immediately
  following this statement
```

Now, you can use a, b, and c as though they were the numbers they stand for:
```
> a+b;
```

$$8 \tag{5}$$

```
> c*a;
```

$$\frac{32}{7} \tag{6}$$

Very important: You must `always` use the asterisk (*) for multiplication -- it is easy to forget it in expressions like `sin(2*x)` or `4*x^3` -- but forgetting the asterisk usually results in a syntax error. It can also result in unexpected (wrong) output -- as when you type `sin(ax)` instead of `sin(a*x)`. Maple 12 relaxes this rule a bit, especially for things like 2x or 3y, but to indicate the product of two variables, the * is still requires; for example, Maple would treat **ab** as a nwe variabe rather than as the product of **a** and **b** which must be typed as **a*b** .

Subtraction uses the minus sign (–) and division the slash (/). To raise a number to a power use the carat (^ shift 6). Maple follows the usual "precedence" rules of arithmetic -- unless parentheses indicate otherwise, Maple exponentiates first, then multiplies and divides from left to right, then adds and subtracts from left to right. Can you predict the output of the following?
```
>  3+4^2-5*2;
```
$$9 \tag{7}$$

Seeing what variables stand for A useful kind of statement is one where you simply type a variable name and a semicolon -- Maple will tell you what the variable stands for. If Maple just returns the variable name, then (usually) the variable has nothing assigned to it.
```
> a;
```
$$3 \tag{8}$$

```
> x;
```
$$x \tag{9}$$

Subsequent assignments affect previous ones If **y** is specified as depending on **x**, and then **x** is assigned a value, then this value of **x** gets substituted into **y**. For example:
```
> y:=sqrt(x+3);
```
$$y := \sqrt{x+3} \tag{10}$$

```
> x:=sin(w);
```
$$x := \sin(w) \tag{11}$$

```
> y;
```
$$\sqrt{\sin(w)+3} \tag{12}$$

And if **x** gets changed, **y** will also change (because Maple remembers the original definition):
```
> x:=cos(t);
```
$$x := \cos(t) \tag{13}$$

```
> y;
```
$$\sqrt{\cos(t)+3} \tag{14}$$

If you get "tangled up" in such assignments, it is possible to "un-assign" a variable. To do this for **x**, type:
```
> x:='x';
```
$$x := x \tag{15}$$

Then x is back to not having any value, and so y is given once again in terms of x:

17

```
> y;
```

$$\sqrt{x+3} \qquad \qquad (16)$$

There are some instances when you want to continue working in the same file, but get rid of all definitions of variables, loaded programs, etc.. To do this, you can type:

```
> restart;
> y;
```

$$y \qquad \qquad (17)$$

Notice that the value of y has now been erased.

Parentheses. Maple uses grouping symbols for specific purposes. There are parentheses ( ), brackets [ ] and braces { }. In general:

Parentheses ( ) are used for grouping algebraic expressions together (as in `2*(x+4)^3` for example), and for delimiting the arguments of functions (as in `sin(x)`, etc..). Neither brackets nor braces may be used for this purpose (their use will result in a syntax error or some other unexpected result).

Brackets [ ] are used for delimiting "ordered lists" -- such as the ordered pair of numbers used to specify a point in the xy-plane. Brackets are also used for defining vectors and matrices, and for "selecting" things from lists (see the section on `solve` for an example of this).

Braces { } are used for delimiting sets, just as in ordinary math. Their most common use is for grouping expressions together when using Maple commands like `plot` or `solve`.

Basic functions that Maple knows Maple has all the standard mathematical functions in its library -- it knows about trig functions, exponentials, logarithms, basic probablity distributions, and many other familiar (and obscure) functions. The function names Maple knows are:

Trig and inverse trig functions `sin, cos, tan, cot, sec, csc, arcsin, arccos, arctan, arccot, arcsec, arccsc`
Hyperbolic functions `sinh, cosh, ..... ,arcsinh,` etc...
Exponential and logarithm Use `exp(x)` for "e to the x". Both `log(x)` and `ln(x)` stand for the natural logarithm -- to get logs to other bases, use e.g. `log[10](x)` for log base 10 of x (this is another use of square brackets).
Square roots, etc `sqrt(x)` stands for the square root of x, `abs(x)` for the absolute value of x.

You can see a longer list of functions Maple knows about using the Help browser (Contents under the Help menu) via the path Mathematics -> Basic Mathematics ->

Initially known functions.

You can define your own functions Say for example you found yourself using the expression $\sqrt{1+x^2}$ all the time, plugging values into it, etc.. You might begin to wish that Maple had a built-in function that was $\sqrt{1+x^2}$. It doesn't, but you can define one yourself, as follows:
```
> f:=x->sqrt(1+x^2);
```
$$f := x \rightarrow \sqrt{1+x^2} \tag{18}$$

The arrow in the input is made with the minus and the greater-than signs. This function definition is a special kind of assignment statement. After doing this, you can use the name **f** in the same way you use **exp** or **sin** or **log**:
```
> f(3*x+1);
```
$$\sqrt{2+9x^2+6x} \tag{19}$$

..and so forth. It is important to realize that you should NEVER, NEVER, NEVER try to define a function with an assignment statement like:
```
> f(x):= sqrt(x+2);
```
$$f(x) := \sqrt{x+2} \tag{20}$$
```
> f(2);
```
$$\sqrt{5} \tag{21}$$

Maple will let you do it, but the resulting **f(x)** will be USELESS -- you can't substitute into it or do anything with it that you normally do with functions. NEVER make assignments like this.   Note that in the example above, Maple returned the value given by the correctly defined function a few lines up [i.e., from f:=x->sqrt(1+x^2); from the output line numbered (18)].

`Important things to  remember about functions and parentheses:` It is `essential`   to remember to use parentheses to delimit the argument of a function -- even though in handwritten math we sometimes cheat and write sin x instead of sin(x), this is not permitted in Maple. Nested parentheses are permitted -- as in
```
> sin(sqrt(x+2)+ln(abs(x)));
```
$$\sin\left(\sqrt{x+2} + \ln(|x|)\right) \tag{22}$$
```
>
```

It is important that the parentheses be matched, i.e., that there are just as many left parentheses as right ones.

Special constants that Maple knows: Maple knows about several standard mathematical constants -- to see which ones, you can type
```
> constants;
```
$$\textit{false}, \gamma, \infty, \textit{true}, \textit{Catalan}, \textit{FAIL}, \pi \tag{23}$$

The names of these constants in Maple input are
```
> false, gamma, infinity, true, Catalan, FAIL, Pi;
```
$$\text{false, } \gamma, \infty, \text{ true, Catalan, FAIL, } \pi \qquad\qquad (24)$$

Maple is case-sensitive -- that is, it is important to put capital and lower-case letters where they belong. For example, Maple knows that
```
> sin(Pi);
```
$$0 \qquad\qquad (25)$$

because it recognizes Pi (with a capital "P") as the famous mathematical constant, but
```
> sin(pi);
```
$$\sin(\pi) \qquad\qquad (26)$$

because Maple recognizes pi (with a little "P") as a variable that happens to have the name π.

Names to avoid: There are many commands and special objects in Maple that have pre-assigned names. There are some that are used so frequently (and, without your knowledge because they occur as part of the internal workings of Maple) that you must never assign any other value to their names. The following are names you should never use:

and	by	D	do	done	elif
else					
end	equation	fi	for	from	if	in
intersect	list	local	matrix	minus	mod
not					
od	option	options	or	proc	quit
read					
save	stop	then	to	union	vector
while					

Nor can the following names be used:

cos	exp	I	ln	log	Pi
sin					
string	tan				

and there are others -- if you think you may be treading on dangerous ground with your names (or if Maple begins to behave mysteriously and you think it may be due to some name conflict), you can type
```
> ?name
```
where name is the name you would like to check -- if you get a Maple help screen for the name, it is probably a good idea to avoid using it.
```
> ?beeblebrox
```

This results in the message:
"Could not find any help on beeblebrox"
which shows that the name "beeblebrox" is probably safe.

Some Notes on Maple's Input Styles

Most of the Maple inputs in this manual use the "traditional" Maple Input style since it shows (almost) all of the keystrokes/characters required to enter data into Maple. Recent versions have a more "math like" input format in which fractions are entered in the standard form of numerator over denominator reather than the one line format where numerators are entered first followed by a "/" character then the deniominator (even though the keystroke sequence is the same--this is a matter of how the fraction or other item is displayed) and exponents when entered appear as they would if you wer writing them on paper. For instance, if a fraction is entered as f:=x/3; in the "traditional format," in Maple 12 you will press the same sequence of keys, but the input looks like a fraction:

> $f := \dfrac{x}{3}$

$$f := \frac{1}{3} x \tag{27}$$

The problem is that once you want to exit the denominator of the fraction to type additional parts of the expression (the same is true for exponents, for instance), you must press the right arrow key to return to the "baseline" for input. For example, to enter x/3+9, you would typr x. /, 3, ->, + 9:

> $g := \dfrac{x}{3} + 9$ # *right arrow was pressed after typing the 3*

$$g := \frac{1}{3} x + 9 \tag{28}$$

>

If you are typing an exponent, for instance and want to type x^2+3x-9, but forget to press the right arrow after the 2, this is what you will get:

> $h := x^{2 + 3x - 9}$

$$h := x^{-7 + 3x} \tag{29}$$

note that the linear term appears in the exponent as does 2-9; the correct entry (pressing the right arrow after entering the 2 for "squared") gives:

> $h := x^2 + 3x - 9$

$$h := x^2 + 3x - 9 \tag{30}$$

which is the desired result.

FOr most of this manual, the "traditional" input style will be use to emphasize what must be typed.

Maple syntax

The most common kind of mistake to make when using Maple is a syntax error. This section reviews the basics of Maple syntax and demonstrates several common syntax errors and how to recover from them.

Don't forget the semi-colon where needed--this is the most common cause of syntax errors!

Rule 1, of course, is that every Maple statement must end with a semi-colon or a colon. If you forget to end a statement with a semi-colon/colon, Maple may warn you about this and, in effect, put a semi-colon at the end of whatever you have typed. If the statement is correct it will be executed; if not, you can go back, edit the statement to correct/complete it, and put in the semicolon.

```
>  restart:
>  int(x^2,x)
Warning, inserted missing semicolon at end of statement
```

$$\frac{1}{3} x^3 \tag{1}$$

Maple 12 is a bit friendlier than earlier versions--it assumes that hitting the return key means you really meant to end the statement and execute it. Earlier versions of Maple just gave an error message or warning about a "missing semi-colon" and at this point you could go back and insert the semicolon.

Match your parentheses! (Brackets and braces, too!)

In Maple statements, there must be a right parenthesis for every left parenthesis, a right bracket for every left bracket and a right brace for every left one and in the proper order. For instance:

```
> plot(x^2,x=-2..2;
Error, `;` unexpected
```

Maple gives you an error message--which says nothing about a missing paren--and puts the cursor back on the statement at the point at which the statement ceased to be syntactically correct. In this example, this point happens to be where the right parenthesis is needed. Sometimes, however, the cursor may not be in the place where the correction needs to be made. For instance, suppose you are trying to assign the expression `(x-3)*sin(x)` to the variable y, but you mistakenly type:

```
> y:=(x-3*sin(x);
Error, `;` unexpected
```

The statement could have made sense all the way up to the semi-colon (but because of the unbalanced parentheses, the statement cannot end there); Maple indicates that something is wrong, but it does not tell where the missing parenthesis should go (indeed, there is no way for Maple to tell since there are multiple possibilities--putting it after the 3 or after sin(x) both make sense mathematically).

Don't forget the * for multiplication...

A common mistake is to forget the asterisk for multiplication. The * is required whenever multiplication is to be performed between two variables or within the parentheses next to a command. It is especially easy to forget this when writing Maple for what in standard notation looks like sin(2x) or something similar. Maple generally requires you to write `sin(2*x)`, although Maple 12 is somewhat more forgiving in that it will sometimes recognize what you mean (but not this time)

```
> sin(2x);
Error, missing operator or `;`
```

Grouping lists of things to plot or equations to solve with braces...

Another common error is to forget the braces when plotting several curves in the same picture, or solving several equations simultaneously:

```
> plot(x^2,x^3,x=-1..1);
Error, (in plot) invalid arguments
```

This means that Maple has construed the three arguments to plot as being "x^2", "x^3" and "x=-1..1". The second of these, "x^3" is not a valid second argument, because the second argument to plot must be a range (like "x=-1..1") or some other indication of how to do the plot. What to plot must be indicated by the first argument only. Therefore, to plot several things at once, you must group them together with braces so that the first argument becomes a set of things to plot:

```
> plot({x^2,x^3},x=-1..1,color=black);
```

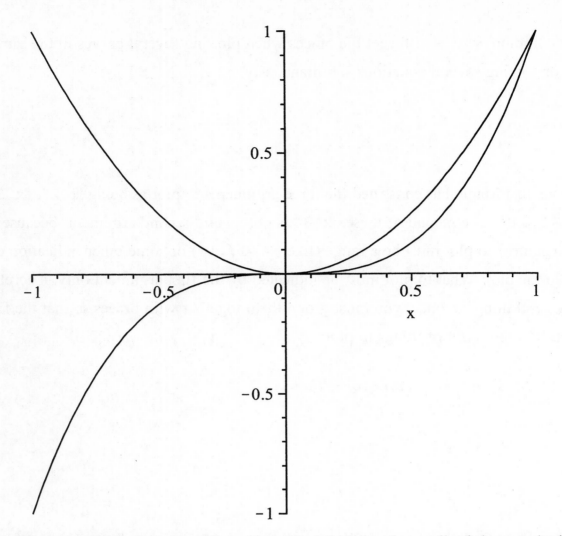

That's better. The "color=black" option tells Maple to draw all of the graphs in black. Maple usually uses colors to distinguish among different functions being plotted, but there is no color in this manual, so...

The same applies to solve:

```
> solve(x+y=1,x-y=2);
```
Error, (in solve) invalid arguments

This is the same problem -- the second argument to solve (which is optional) is the list of variables to solve for. The equations must be in the first argument, so if there are several equations to be solved simultaneously, they must be grouped together using braces:

```
> solve({x+y=1,x-y=2});
```

$$\left\{ y = \frac{-1}{2}, x = \frac{3}{2} \right\} \tag{2}$$

```
>  x := rhs(%[1]); y := rhs(%%[2]);
```

$$x := \frac{-1}{2}$$

$$y := \frac{3}{2} \tag{3}$$

It is important to remember that the values of the variables are not assigned to them by the solve statement. The second statement (x:=, etc, assigns the answers from solve to variables x and y. The "rhs" command selects the right hand side of an equality. the [1] and [2] select either the first or second, respectively, entries in the list of solutions, and the % signs select the previous output. Two %s are used to select the y value as the first rhs command will have an output (x:=...), so the list becomes the second output back, requiring 2 % signs to designate it. If that sounds complicated, it is, but a little study will show you how the %, %% and %%% "remember" refrences work. Note that Maple only remembers the last three outputs, so there is no %%%% reference available.

Misspellings

Usually, if you spell the name of a command incorrectly, no syntax error will result. Maple will just assume that you meant to use a command that has yet to be specified:

```
>  x:='x':y:='y':solbe(x^2+x=4,x);
```

$$solbe\left(x^2 + x = 4, x \right) \tag{4}$$

You can see that Maple just parrots back the input, because it has no way of interpreting it. When this happens, it is ok simply to retype the statement correctly, or even to place the cursor back on the incorrect statement, correct the error, and try again:

```
>  solve(x^2+x=4);
```

$$-\frac{1}{2} + \frac{1}{2}\sqrt{17}, -\frac{1}{2} - \frac{1}{2}\sqrt{17} \tag{5}$$

Since x is the only variable in the problem, Maple assumes that you want to solve for.

Seems obvious--and to a human, it is--but Maple is a program and can only respond to things for which it has been programmed. If there are two or more variables you must tell Maple for which of them you wish to solve.

$$solve(\{x+y=6,x-y=0\},\{x,y\});$$

$$\{x=3, y=3\}$$

Commands contained in special libraries...

Some of the commands we will use are contained in special libraries that are not read in automatically when you start Maple (because there are too many of them). For example, the commands
"DEplot", "DEplot3d", etc.. for illustrating "slope fields" of differential equations are contained in the "DEtools" library. To read these commands into the computer's memory, you must use a "with" statement. If you forget to do this, Maple will respond as though you misspelled a command:

```
> DEplot(diff(y(x),x)=y(x)+x^2,y(x),x=1..4,[[y(0)=-1]],y=-5..5);
```

$$DEplot\left(\frac{d}{dx} y(x) = y(x) + x^2, y(x), x = 1..4, [[y(0) = -1]], y = -5..5 \right) \qquad (6)$$

When Maple parrots a command like this, and you have ascertained that you spelled the command correctly, then consider whether you need to read the command in from a library. For example, to get the DEplot command:

```
> with(DEtools,DEplot); # reads ONLY DEplot rather than the entire
  library of commands--saves wasting memory on commands you won't
  use
```

$$[DEplot] \qquad (7)$$

```
> DEplot(diff(y(x),x)=y(x)+x^2,y(x),x=1..4,[[y(0)=-1]],y=-5..5);
  #this works now and produces the desired plot:
```

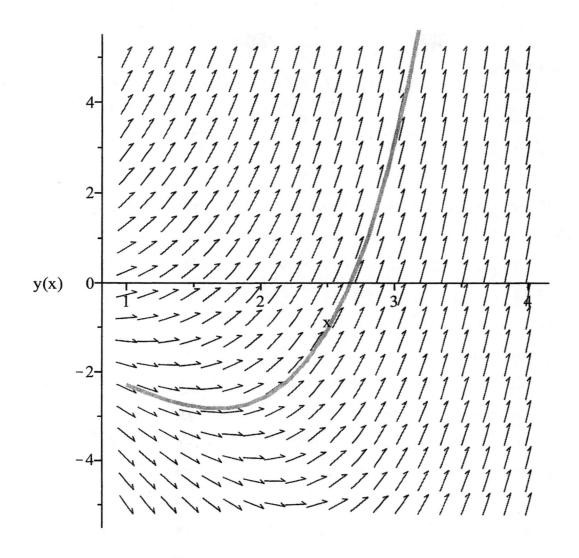

>

The syntax here is:

```
    with("name of library", "name(s) of command(s) separated
by commas if there are several");
```

If you want to read in the entire contents of a library (we do this occasionally with the student library and others), then with(<Library Name>); will do this.

Here is a partial list of the various libraries we will use in Math 240 and 241 with their contents. The commands of interest from each of these will be discussed and examples given later in this manual. For information about other commands in these lbraries use the Maple Help system. The libraries and their contents are:

DEtools library:

> *with*(*DEtools*);

[*AreSimilar, DEnormal, DEplot, DEplot3d, DEplot_polygon, DFactor,*   **(8)**

    DFactorLCLM, DFactorsols, Dchangevar, FunctionDecomposition, GCRD,

    Gosper, Heunsols, Homomorphisms, IsHyperexponential, LCLM, MeijerGsols,

    MultiplicativeDecomposition, PDEchangecoords, PolynomialNormalForm,

    RationalCanonicalForm, ReduceHyperexp, RiemannPsols, Xchange,

    Xcommutator, Xgauge, Zeilberger, abelsol, adjoint, autonomous, bernoullisol,

    buildsol, buildsym, canoni, caseplot, casesplit, checkrank, chinisol, clairautsol,

    constcoeffsols, convertAlg, convertsys, dalembertsol, dcoeffs, de2diffop,

    dfieldplot, diff_table, diffop2de, dperiodic_sols, dpolyform, dsubs, eigenring,

    endomorphism_charpoly, equinv, eta_k, eulersols, exactsol, expsols,

    exterior_power, firint, firtest, formal_sol, gen_exp, generate_ic, genhomosol,

    gensys, hamilton_eqs, hypergeomsols, hyperode, indicialeq, infgen, initialdata,

    integrate_sols, intfactor, invariants, kovacicsols, leftdivision, liesol, line_int,

    linearsol, matrixDE, matrix_riccati, maxdimsystems, moser_reduce, muchange,

    mult, mutest, newton_polygon, normalG2, ode_int_y, ode_y1, odeadvisor,

    odepde, parametricsol, particularsol, phaseportrait, poincare, polysols,

    power_equivalent, ratsols, redode, reduceOrder, reduce_order, regular_parts,

    regularsp, remove_RootOf, riccati_system, riccatisol, rifread, rifsimp,

    rightdivision, rtaylor, separablesol, singularities, solve_group, super_reduce,

    symgen, symmetric_power, symmetric_product, symtest, transinv, translate,

    untranslate, varparam, zoom]

The most used commands here will be DEplot and DEplot3d plus odeadvisor.

The plotting libraries will be quite useful, especially for 3D or other complex graphs

> *with*(*plots*); *with*(*plottools*);

[*animate, animate3d, animatecurve, arrow, changecoords, complexplot, complexplot3d,*

    conformal, conformal3d, contourplot, contourplot3d, coordplot, coordplot3d, densityplot,

    display, dualaxisplot, fieldplot, fieldplot3d, gradplot, gradplot3d, graphplot3d, implicitplot,

    implicitplot3d, inequal, interactive, interactiveparams, intersectplot, listcontplot,

listcontplot3d, listdensityplot, listplot, listplot3d, loglogplot, logplot, matrixplot, multiple,
odeplot, pareto, plotcompare, pointplot, pointplot3d, polarplot, polygonplot, polygonplot3d,
polyhedra_supported, polyhedraplot, rootlocus, semilogplot, setcolors, setoptions,
setoptions3d, spacecurve, sparsematrixplot, surfdata, textplot, textplot3d, tubeplot]

[*arc, arrow, circle, cone, cuboid, curve, cutin, cutout, cylinder, disk, dodecahedron, ellipse,*   **(9)**
ellipticArc, hemisphere, hexahedron, homothety, hyperbola, icosahedron, line, octahedron,
parallelepiped, pieslice, point, polygon, project, rectangle, reflect, rotate, scale, semitorus,
sphere, stellate, tetrahedron, torus, transform, translate, vrml]

The *plots* animation commands (animate, animate3d) are useful for dynamic illustrations of various mathematical ideas, plot3d and tubeplot are used for 3D plotting and the implicitplot commands are used when putting the expression to be graphed into y=f(x) form is difficult or impossible. *plottools* contains commands for drawing a number of geometric figures and useful symbols.

Another useful set of commands is in the vector calculus library:
>   *with*(*VectorCalculus*);
[*&x, `*`, `+`, `-`, `.`, <,>, </>, About, AddCoordinates, ArcLength,*   **(10)**
BasisFormat, Binormal, Compatibility, ConvertVector, CrossProd,
CrossProduct, Curl, Curvature, D, *Del, DirectionalDiff, Divergence, DotProd,*
DotProduct, Flux, GetCoordinateParameters, GetCoordinates, GetNames,
GetPVDescription, GetRootPoint, GetSpace, Gradient, Hessian,
IsPositionVector, IsRootedVector, IsVectorField, Jacobian, Laplacian, LineInt,
MapToBasis, Nabla, Norm, Normalize, PathInt, PlotPositionVector,
PlotVector, PositionVector, PrincipalNormal, RadiusOfCurvature,
RootedVector, ScalarPotential, SetCoordinateParameters, SetCoordinates,
SpaceCurve, SurfaceInt, TNBFrame, Tangent, TangentLine, TangentPlane,
TangentVector, Torsion, Vector, VectorField, VectorPotential, VectorSpace,
Wronskian, diff, eval, evalVF, int, limit, series]

See the section of the manual discussing these commands for more information.

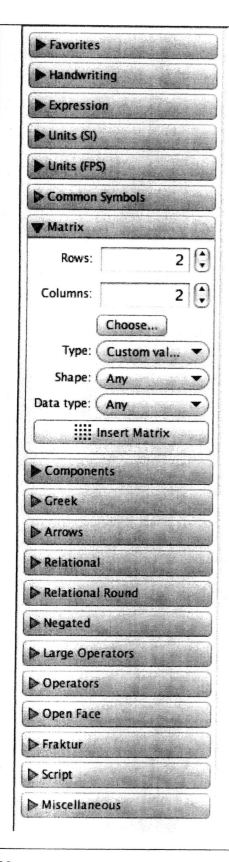

Palettes

Palettes make it easier for the user to handle some of Maple's more complicated syntax by giving the user a template for the input of such functions as int and diff. In addition, the symbol palettes make it easier for the user to insert various mathematical symbols into his worksheets. Maple also has matrix palettes which work similarly to expression palettes. In Maple 12, the list of available palettes is in the left column of the worksheet. Palettes include the symbol and expression palettes discussed below as well as a large number of additional palettes for matrices, common symbols and relational operators. Maple 12 even includes a (rudimentary) "handwriting" recognition palette-- see the Maple Help system for more details.

Symbol Palettes

To use the symbol palette, you must open it. To do this, click on the arrowhead next to the "Common Symbols" palette name in the left column of the worksheet window. Once you are in the midst of typing an expression, you can use the symbol palette as follows:

1. In the expression, click on the location (placeholder) where you want to insert the symbol.

2. On the Symbol Palette, click on the symbol you want to enter; for example, to enter an alpha symbol, click on . Note that besides Greek letters, you can also use the symbol pallette to insert e, Pi, infinity and the complex number i.

When you click on a button on the palette, the mathematical symbol (if you are using Standard Math notation) or character name (if you are using Maple notation) is entered at the currently selected placeholder.

Expression Palettes

Entering a Palette Expression

To enter a palette expression, follow these steps:
  1. Click on the location (Maple prompt or placeholder) where you want to enter the operation.
  2. Click on the operation you want to enter; for example, for division, click on .
  3. Fill in placeholders by entering numbers, symbols, or expressions.

Press the Tab key to move the cursor from placeholder to placeholder. If no more empty placeholders remain, the cursor moves to the end of the line. If you are using Maple notation, type a semicolon and press Enter to execute the expression.
For example:
To enter the expression for the integral of x^2 for x from 0 to 2, we would do the following:
`int(%?, %?=%?..%?);` #click on the definite integral icon in the Expression palette
`int(x^2, x=0..2);` #press the TAB key to move between placeholders
(designated by %?), entering the appropriate expressions/values as needed. Pressing the RETURN or ENTER key evaluates the expression:

$$\frac{8}{3}$$

Note: If you want to have symbol, expression, or matrix as part of your text, while you are in the text mode, hit F5 key, a placeholder will appear for you to select your symbol, expression, or matrix from the appropriate palette. Hit F5 key again to return to the text mode.

Expressions vs. Functions vs. Programs in Maple

One issue that often causes confusion is the distinction Maple makes between "expressions" and "functions". Sometimes, the same confusion exists in ordinary mathematics, between "variables" and "functions". The idea is pretty straightforward, but can be hard to keep track of sometimes.

For example, suppose you want y to be x^2. There are two senses (in mathematics and in Maple) in which this can be taken. First, you may simply want y to be a variable that represents the square of whatever x happens to be. Then in Maple, you would write:
```
> restart:
> y:=x^2;
```
$$y := x^2 \tag{1}$$
(In mathematics, you'd write pretty much the same thing, perhaps without the colon). This defines y to be the *expression* x^2. The other thing you might mean is that y should represent a *function* that transforms any number (or variable) into its square. Then in Maple you would write:
```
> y:=x->x^2;
```
$$y := x \rightarrow x^2 \tag{2}$$
You read this as "y maps x to x squared". In ordinary math, you would probably write y (x)=x^2, more or less.

In calculus classes, we are often casual (almost to the point of being careless) about the distinction between variables and functions. This is one reason the chain rule for derivatives can be so confusing. Maple, however, forces us to be explicit about whether we are using expressions or functions. Most of the time, we can accomplish what we want to do with either of them (although the way we have to do things can be somewhat different, as illustrated below), but occasionally we are forced to use one or the other.

We look at several (most, actually) of the operations you will need to apply to functions and expressions -- sometimes, we will use commands that are described elsewhere in this manual without too much explanation; you can find more complete explanations in the sections dealing with these commands. The operations we will look at are: substituting a value (or other expression) for x into y, solving equations involving y, applying calculus operations (limit, derivative and integral) to y, and plotting the graph of y.

EXPRESSIONS

Even though it is not such an interesting expression, we will go through all of the operations on the expression x^2. So all of the examples below assume that the statement

```
>  y:=x^2;
```

$$y := x^2 \tag{3}$$

has been executed first.

1. **Plugging in**: To plug a number (or other expression) in for x and evaluate y, the command `subs` (short for substitute) is used. The syntax is explained fully in the section on the `subs` command. Here is a simple example:

```
>  subs(x=8,y);
```

$$64 \tag{4}$$

It is possible to make substitutions of one variable for another as well:

```
>  subs(x=f,y);
```

$$f^2 \tag{5}$$

You can even substitute expressions involving x for x -- such as when you calculate derivatives by the definition (i.e., the long way):

```
>  subs(x = x + h,y);
```

$$(x+h)^2 \tag{6}$$

The important thing to remember about subs is that it has NO EFFECT on y at all. It just reports what the result would be if you make the substitution. So even after all the statements above, the value of y is still:

```
>  y;
```

$$x^2 \tag{7}$$

2. **Solving equations** One helpful use of expressions is that they save typing. You can use the name of an expression in its place anywhere you might need to type the expression. Not that `x^2` is so onerous to type, but you can imagine more substantial uses. To solve quadratic equations (for instance `x^2=5`), we can type `y` instead of `x^2`, as follows:

```
>  solve(y=5);
```

$$\sqrt{5}, -\sqrt{5} \tag{8}$$

This works (of course) with `fsolve`, too:

```
>  fsolve(y=5);
```

$$-2.236067977, 2.236067977 \tag{9}$$

Here is a more sophisticated example (note that we have to tell Maple what variable we are solving for because there are more than one--remember that y=x^2):

```
>  solve(y=a^2+4*a+4,x);
```

$$-a-2, a+2 \tag{10}$$

3. **Calculus operations**: The syntax for calculus operations is just as described in their respective sections. For instance to calculate the limit of `x^2` as x approaches 5, we would type:

```
>  limit(y,x=5);
```

$$25 \tag{11}$$

Or the derivative of `x^2`:
```
> diff(y,x);
```

$$2\,x \tag{12}$$

Or the indefinite integral:
```
> int(y,x);
```

$$\frac{1}{3}\,x^3 \tag{13}$$

Or a definite one:
```
> int(y,x=-2..2);
```

$$\frac{16}{3} \tag{14}$$

4. **Plotting.** To plot the graph of y, the standard syntax of the plot statement is used:

```
> plot(y,x=-4..4);
```

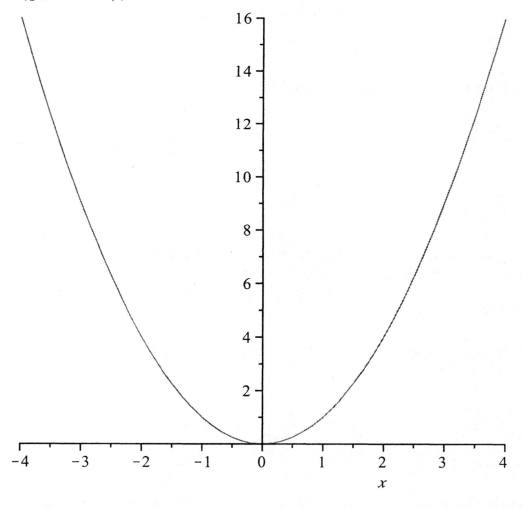

An important aspect (which contrasts with using functions) is that the variable appears in the specification of the domain (i.e., the "x" in x=-4..4).

In general, expressions are easier to define and use than functions, as we shall now see:

FUNCTIONS

Again, we'll stick with defining y to be x^2. But this time we're assuming that y has been defined as a function, via the statement:
```
> y:=x->x^2;
```
$$y := x \rightarrow x^2 \tag{15}$$

1. **Plugging in**: This is the one operation that is actually easier for functions. Since the definition of y is now:
```
> y;
```
$$y \tag{16}$$

invisible to the usual way of looking at variables (because y is not a variable, it is a function). But you can look at the definition of y using the notation of standard mathematics:
```
> y(x);
```
$$x^2 \tag{17}$$

Since y is a function, we can use other letters or expressions in place of x in y(x):
```
> y(t);
```
$$t^2 \tag{18}$$
```
> y(5);
```
$$25 \tag{19}$$
```
> y(x+h);
```
$$(x+h)^2 \tag{20}$$

You get the idea.

2. **Solving equations**: To solve an equation involving a function, you need to plug in a variable in order to convert it to an expression, because equations have expressions on either side of the equals sign. (Note that y is a function, but y(x) is an expression):
```
> solve(y=2,x);
```

This gives no output because y is a function, not an expression. We should type instead:
```
> solve(y(x)=2,x);
```
$$\sqrt{2}, -\sqrt{2} \tag{21}$$

It is the same with fsolve:
```
> fsolve(y(x)=17,x=3..5);
```
$$4.123105626 \tag{22}$$

(See the fsolve section of this manual for the rest of the syntax here).

3. **Calculus**: Maple actually has a special command for taking derivatives of functions (but none for limits or integrals). It is called D. You don't need (in fact, you shouldn't use) the y(x) notation with D, just y:
```
> D(y);
```
$$\tag{23}$$

$$x \rightarrow 2\,x \tag{23}$$

Notice that the result of D is another function (here, the function that maps x to `2*x`) rather than an expression, as is the case with `diff`.

For integrals and limits, you must use the `y(x)` notation as with equations. It is also possible to use `diff` with the `y(x)` notation. Here are some examples:
First, one that doesn't work:
```
> limit(y,x=3);
```

$$y \tag{24}$$

(See why we need the `y(x)` notation?)
```
> limit(y(x),x=3);
```

$$9 \tag{25}$$

```
> diff(y(x),x);
```

$$2\,x \tag{26}$$

Of course, one advantage of functions is that we can also do:
```
> diff(y(t),t);
```

$$2\,t \tag{27}$$

if we need to. Finally, for integrals:
```
> int(y(x),x);
```

$$\frac{1}{3}\,x^3 \tag{28}$$

```
> int(y(q),q=1..4);
```

$$21 \tag{29}$$

4. **Plotting** There are two ways to do plotting of functions. The first is the usual way as for expressions, and works the same as the calculus rules with `y(x)`:

```
> plot(y(x),x=-3..3);
```

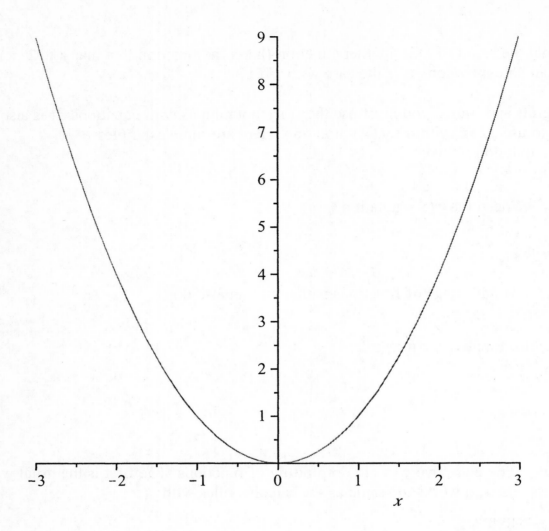

No surprises here -- all of the usual plotting options and tricks are available for functions this way.

One new wrinkle is that a function can be plotted without using the y(x) notation, but the syntax is slightly different: Since no variable is specified in the notation, no variable can be specified for the domain (otherwise an "empty plot" will result). Here is the proper syntax:

```
> plot(y,-3..3);
```

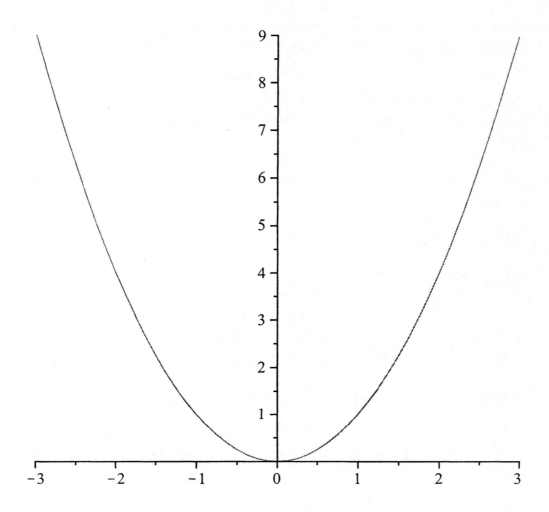

Compare this graph with the one above -- there is one subtle difference (the x-axis isn't labelled).

That's basically it, as far as functions and expressions are concerned. The idea of using functions opens up a major new part of the Maple system -- the fact that in addition to being a "calculus calculator", it is also a *programming language* . Yes, you can write programs in Maple. This will occasionally be useful, because occasionally you will need to apply some procedure (like taking the derivative and setting it equal to zero) over and over, and you will get tired of typing the same thing all the time. You can create your own extensions to the Maple language in this way.

Our purpose here is not to teach Maple programming, but here are a few basics and an example or two so you see how it's done. There are several examples of Maple programs in the demonstrations. You can copy and paste them in your homework assignments if you find this useful (you will, occasionally).

A Maple program (actually called a "procedure") is created by a Maple statement containing the `proc` command. A simple example is the following:

```
> y:=proc(x) x^2 end;
```

$$y := \mathbf{proc}(x)\ x^2\ \mathbf{end\ proc} \tag{30}$$

This statement is in fact equivalent to `y:=x->x^2` . In fact, Maple translates `y:= x->x^2` into the above statement. It illustrates most of the basic parts of a Maple program:

1. `y:=` -- it is necessary to give your program a name. You do this by assigning the procedure to a variable name.

2. `proc` -- This tells Maple that you are writing a program.

3. `(x)` -- You put the names of the input to the program in parentheses. In this case, the program takes one item of input, the number `x`.

4. `x^2` -- This is the statement that will be executed when the program is run. There can be many statements in a procedure. They are separated by semicolons, as usual.

5. `end;` -- All programs must end with an **end** statement; otherwise, how is Maple to know you're done?

Once the program is defined, you can use it just as you would any Maple command:

```
> y(20);
```

$$400 \tag{31}$$

and so forth...

A more interesting program is the following one, which looks for critical points (it doesn't always work, though).

```
> crit:=proc(f) local d;
    d:=diff(f,x);
    print(solve(d= 0,x),` is a critical point of `,f);
  end;
```

$$crit := \mathbf{proc}(f) \tag{32}$$
$$\mathbf{local}\ d;\ d := \mathit{diff}\,(f, x);\ \mathit{print}(\mathit{solve}(d = 0,\ x),\ \textit{is a critical point of}\,, f)$$
$$\mathbf{end\ proc}$$

Notice that Maple parrots back the definition of the function. This function needed two statements, and has a "local" variable. To get more than one line in your definition of a function, you need to use the SHIFT+ENTER keys together between lines, and just plain ENTER at the end.

The "`local`" variable means that "d" is declared to be a "private" variable for the purposes of the program -- so the use of `d` here will NOT interfere with any other definition of `d` that may be in your worksheet but outside of the program. Local variables must be declared at the beginning of the program, and a semi-colon must follow the list of local variables.

The other new thing here is the "`print`" statement. When we use the program "`crit`", you will be able to figure out what the `print` statement does:

```
> crit(x^2+2*x);
```

$$-1, \; \textit{is a critical point of}, \; x^2 + 2\,x \qquad\qquad (33)$$

So the value of `d` (calculated in the first statement of the program) is printed, followed by the character string `` `is a critical point of` `` (note that both of the quotes that surround a character string are LEFT quotes -- on the keyboard to the left of the digit 1), and then the input expression is printed.

A TINY BIT OF PROGRAMMING: We can improve `crit` so that it checks to see if the critical point is a local max or a local min using the second derivative test, as follows:

```
> crit:=proc(y) local d, dd, c;
     d:=diff(y,x);
  c:=solve(d=0,x);
  print(c,` is a critical point of `,y);
  dd:=diff(d,x);
  if subs(x=c,dd)>0 then print(`It is a local minimum.`)
     elif subs(x=c,dd)<0 then print(`It is a local maximum.`)
     else
       print(`The second derivative test is inconclusive for this
  point.`) fi;
  end;
```

$$crit := \mathbf{proc}(\,y\,) \qquad\qquad (34)$$

$$\mathbf{local}\ d,\, dd,\, c;$$
$$d := \textit{diff}\,(\,y,\, x\,);$$
$$c := \textit{solve}(\,d = 0,\, x\,);$$
$$\textit{print}(\,c,\ \textit{is a critical point of}\,,\, y\,);$$
$$dd := \textit{diff}\,(\,d,\, x\,);$$
$$\mathbf{if}\ 0 < \textit{subs}(\,x = c,\, dd\,)\ \mathbf{then}$$
$$\qquad \textit{print}(\,\textit{It is a local minimum.}\,)$$
$$\mathbf{elif}\ \textit{subs}(\,x = c,\, dd\,) < 0\ \mathbf{then}$$
$$\qquad \textit{print}(\,\textit{It is a local maximum.}\,)$$
$$\mathbf{else}$$
$$\qquad \textit{print}(\,\textit{The second derivative test is inconclusive for this point.}\,)$$
$$\mathbf{end\ if}$$
$$\mathbf{end\ proc}$$

The fancy thing here is the "`if`" statement. In fact, it is an "`if/then/elif/then/else/fi`" statement! You read "`elif`" as "else, if". The statement embodies the second derivative test: If the second derivative `dd` at the point `c` is positive then `c` is a local minimum, otherwise, if `dd` is negative at `c`, then `c` is a local maximum, otherwise the test is inconclusive. The "`fi`" at the end tells Maple that the `if` statement is over (it is possible to have several statements after each "`then`" and after the "`else`". "`fi`" is "`if`" backwards, sort of like a right parenthesis is to a left one.

Here is the program at work:

```
> crit(x^2+2*x);
```

$$-1, \text{ is a critical point of }, x^2 + 2\,x$$
$$It\ is\ a\ local\ minimum.$$

(35)

```
> crit(x^3+2*x);
```

$$\frac{1}{3}\,\mathrm{I}\sqrt{6}\,,\ -\frac{1}{3}\,\mathrm{I}\sqrt{6}\,,\ \text{is a critical point of },\, x^3 + 2\,x$$

```
Error, (in crit) cannot determine if this expression is true or false: 0 < {
(2*I)*6^(1/2), -(2*I)*6^(1/2)}
```

Uh-oh--we told you it wouldn't always work! This is because x^3+2*x has two (complex!) critical points and our program hasn't made allowances for either the fact that the critical points might not be real or that there might be more than one.

Here is a complete, working version (it still doesn't check for errors in the input, but it's not so bad). You can look in books about Maple for all of the syntax, or find some of it in Maple help:

```
> crit:=proc(y) local d, dd, c, cc;
     d:=diff(y,x);
  c:=solve(d=0,x);
  for cc in c do if type(cc,realcons) then
  print(cc,` is a critical point of `,y);
  dd:=diff(d,x);
  if evalf(subs(x=cc,dd))>0 then print(`It is a local minimum.`)
     elif evalf(subs(x=cc,dd))<0 then print(`It is a local maximum.
  `)
     else
     print(`The second derivative test is inconclusive for this
  point.`) fi;
  fi; od;
  end;
```

$$crit := \mathbf{proc}(y)$$

$$\mathbf{local}\ d,\ dd,\ c,\ cc;$$

$$d := diff(y, x);$$

$$c := solve(d = 0, x);$$

$$\mathbf{for}\ cc\ \mathbf{in}\ c\ \mathbf{do}$$

$$\quad \mathbf{if}\ type(cc, realcons)\ \mathbf{then}$$

$$\qquad print(cc,\ is\ a\ critical\ point\ of, y);$$

$$\qquad dd := diff(d, x);$$

$$\qquad \mathbf{if}\ 0 < evalf(subs(x = cc, dd))\ \mathbf{then}$$

$$\qquad\quad print(It\ is\ a\ local\ minimum.)$$

$$\qquad \mathbf{elif}\ evalf(subs(x = cc, dd)) < 0\ \mathbf{then}$$

$$\qquad\quad print(It\ is\ a\ local\ maximum.)$$

$$\qquad \mathbf{else}$$

$$\qquad\quad print(The\ second\ derivative\ test\ is\ inconclusive\ for\ this\ point.)$$

$$\qquad \mathbf{end\ if}$$

$$\quad \mathbf{end\ if}$$

$$\mathbf{end\ do}$$

$$\mathbf{end\ proc}$$

(36)

It is nice that when Maple parrots the definition of the program, it formats the output so you can see where the various if's and do's begin and end. The "*type*" statement is used to check that the critical points are reals Let's try it out:

First on one that worked before:
```
> crit(x^2+2*x);
```

$$-1, \text{ is a critical point of } , x^2 + 2\,x$$
$$\textit{It is a local minimum.}$$

(37)

Now a better one:

```
> crit(x^3+2*x);
```

No output! That is right, for as we know from before, this function has no real critical points. If we change it a little, it will have two:
```
> crit(x^3-2*x);
```

$$\frac{1}{3}\sqrt{6}, \text{ is a critical point of } , x^3 - 2\,x$$
$$\textit{It is a local minimum.}$$
$$-\frac{1}{3}\sqrt{6}, \text{ is a critical point of } , x^3 - 2\,x$$
$$\textit{It is a local maximum.}$$

(38)

Just as it should be!

One place where you will need to write a program like this is to define "piecewise" functions. Here is an example, from which you can get the idea:
```
> f:=proc(x)
  if x<2 then x-5 else 3-2*x^2 fi
  end;
```

$$f := \mathbf{proc}(x) \text{ if } x < 2 \text{ then } x - 5 \text{ else } 3 - 2*x{\char`\^}2 \text{ end if end proc}$$

(39)

You have to be careful when plotting these. For instance the following won't work:

```
> plot(f(x),x=-1..4);
Error, (in f) cannot determine if this expression is true or false: x < 2
```

However, as indicated in the section of this manual on the plot function, the following does work:
```
> plot(f,-1..4);
```

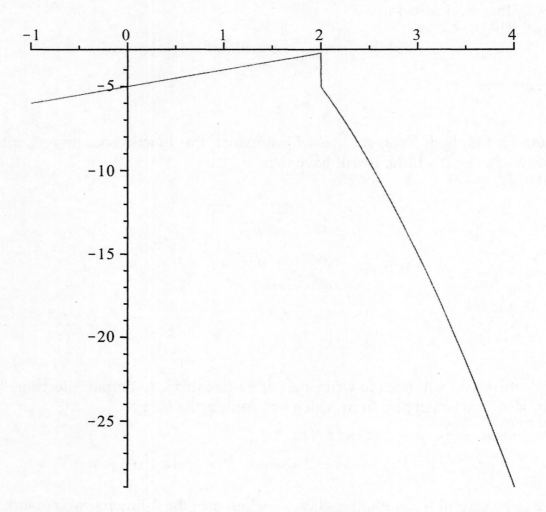

Since f is a discontinuous function, there should be a gap between the two pieces at $x = 2$. Because Maple makes graphs by "connecting the dots," we have to tell Maple that there is at least one discontinuity. To do that, use the "discont=true" option of the plot statement:

```
> plot(f,-1..4,discont=true);
```

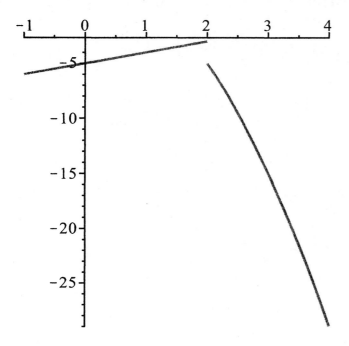

The other programming construction we will use occasionally (even outside of programs) is the "for/from/to/do/od " statement. It is used to make tables of functions and to repeat of a set of commands over and over. For example, a good table of sines and cosines obtained from the following:

```
>  for k from 1 to 8 do k*Pi/4,cos(k*Pi/4),sin(k*Pi/4) od;
```

$$\frac{1}{4} \pi, \frac{1}{2} \sqrt{2}, \frac{1}{2} \sqrt{2}$$

$$\frac{1}{2} \pi, 0, 1$$

$$\frac{3}{4} \pi, -\frac{1}{2} \sqrt{2}, \frac{1}{2} \sqrt{2}$$

$$\pi, -1, 0$$

$$\frac{5}{4} \pi, -\frac{1}{2} \sqrt{2}, -\frac{1}{2} \sqrt{2}$$

$$\frac{3}{2} \pi, 0, -1$$

$$\frac{7}{4} \pi, \frac{1}{2} \sqrt{2}, -\frac{1}{2} \sqrt{2}$$

$$2 \pi, 1, 0$$ (40)

>

You get the idea -- the statement k*Pi/4,cos(k*Pi/4),sin(k*Pi/4) was executed for each value of k from 1 to 8. The "do" and "od" or "end do" are used to

47

surround what is allowed to be a set of several statements. Think of them as a kind of "programming brackets."

solve

The `solve` command in Maple is used, of course, for solving equations and systems of equations.

An equation in Maple is an object which contains an equals sign -- on each side of the equals sign must be a Maple <u>expression</u> (not a function). At least one of the expressions in an equation must contain at least one variable. Some examples of equations are:

```
x^2+5*x=2
3*x+4*y=5*z
1/a + 1/b = 1/c
x^2=sin(x)
```

and so on. An equation can be assigned to a name, as in:

```
> restart:
> eqn:=x^2+5*x=2;
```

$$eqn := x^2 + 5\,x = 2 \tag{1}$$

Then, you can use the Maple commands lhs (for "left-hand side") and rhs (for "right-hand side") to specify the two expressions in the equation, as follows:

```
> lhs(eqn);rhs(eqn);
```

$$x^2 + 5\,x$$
$$2 \tag{2}$$

Using solve to solve a single equation: The syntax of `solve` for one equation is the standard Maple syntax:

```
solve(what,how);
```

In place of "what" goes the equation to be solved (or the name of the equation). "How" in the case of the solve command means "for what variable". In some of the examples above, there is more than one variable, and it is necessary to tell Maple which variable it should solve for. So, examples of valid solve statements would be:

```
> solve(1/a+1/b=1/c,b);
```

$$\frac{a\,c}{-c+a} \tag{3}$$

```
> solve(eqn,x);
```

$$-\frac{5}{2} + \frac{1}{2}\sqrt{33},\ -\frac{5}{2} - \frac{1}{2}\sqrt{33} \tag{4}$$

In this second example, we used the name of the equation instead of typing it out again.

What solve does: The `solve` command attempts to apply the rules of algebra to find an expression which, when substituted for the variable, will satisfy the equation. `Solve` thus returns "exact" mathematical answers, rather than numerical approximations (you can see this in the two examples above). If the logarithm of 17 appears in the solution to the equation being solved, `solve` will print out ln(17) rather than its decimal equivalent.

`Solve` knows that the number of roots of a polynomial equation is equal to its degree. It also knows the quadratic, cubic and quartic formulas, and that there is no general formula for the roots of polynomials of degree 5 or higher. Thus, solve will report all of the roots of a polynomial if it can find them. For transcendental (i.e., non-polynomial) equations, solve will attempt to find a solution, but will not attempt to find all solutions (in fact, many transcendental equations have an infinite number of solutions -- think of the equation sin(x)=exp(-x) -- so it is a good thing that Maple does not attempt to find them all).

The result of solve: Assuming you have input the correct syntax, the result of the `solve` command will be one of the following:

(a) a solution (or solutions) of the equation (which may contain mysterious special functions from advanced mathematics or substitute expressions), or

(b) nothing.

In case (a), it is important to realize several things: The `solve` command simply tells you the answer to the equation. It does not assign the answer to the variable being solved for. For example, in the exchange:

```
> solve(x+4=9,x);
```

$$5 \qquad\qquad (5)$$

the variable `x` has no value after the execution of the solve statement. In general , it is a good idea to assign the result of the solve command to a variable (usually other than the one being solved for). This way, you will have easy access to the solutions for further use (especially if there is more than one).

EXAMPLE:

A falling object is `100-16*t^2` feet above the ground at time `t` seconds. Its velocity at time `t` is `-32*t` feet per second. What is its velocity when it hits the ground?

Solution: First, we need to solve for the time t for which the height is zero. We first define variables h and `v` to represent the height and velocity:

```
> h:=100-16*t^2:   v:=-32*t:
```

Now we solve for when h=0 --

```
> c:=solve(h=0,t);
```

$$c := \frac{-5}{2}, \frac{5}{2} \qquad\qquad (6)$$

There are two solutions, and the variable `c` now stands for the list consisting of the two solutions. To see or use one of the solutions at a time, we can use the expressions `c[1]` and `c[2]`. For example, to substitute the second solution into v (which is what the

51

problem asks for), we can enter:

```
> subs(t=c[2],v);
```

$$-80 \qquad (7)$$

So the velocity at impact is 80 feet per second. (See the section on the `subs` command if you do not understand this last statement).

Some kind of mysterious symbols that can appear come up when you attempt to solve a transcendental equation. This is because Maple knows about several special functions from advanced mathematics, many of which were invented and given names precisely because names were required for the solutions of certain transcendental equations (you have already met examples of these, such as the logarithm and the arcsin functions). Often, in this case, using `evalf` will help, sometimes Maple's help facility will provide useful information concerning the special function being used, and still other times one must resort to the `plot`-and-`fsolve` strategy discussed in the next paragraph.

In case (b), when the solve command returns nothing, this means that either there are no solutions of the equation at all, or that there are no solutions that can be expressed algebraically, or that Maple is unable to find the solution. How you respond to this depends on the particular situation. The most common situation is when you are trying to solve one equation containing one variable and no other unspecified variable names. In this case, the best way to proceed is often to plot the left and right hand sides of the equation over various ranges to see if there are any intersection points (whose x-coordinates are solutions of the equation), and, if you find one, to use `fsolve` to get decimal approximations of the solutions (see the sections on `plot` and `fsolve` for more details). Here is an example:

```
> eqn:=sin(x)=exp(-x);
```

$$eqn := \sin(x) = e^{(-x)} \qquad (8)$$

```
> solve(eqn,x);
```

$$\mathrm{RootOf}(\_Z + \ln(\sin(\_Z))) \tag{9}$$

This unhelpful output indicates that Maple has given up --`solve` cannot find a solution. So, we try plotting:

```
> plot({sin(x),exp(-x)},x=-2..2,color=[red,blue],
  thickness=2);
```

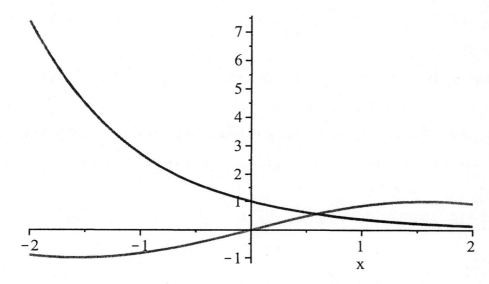

It appears there is a solution for x between zero and one -- so we try fsolving:

```
> fsolve(eqn,x,x=0..1);
```

$$0.5885327440 \tag{10}$$

```
> c:=%; sin(c),exp(-c);
```

$$c := 0.5885327440 \tag{11}$$

$$0.5551412218, 0.5551412217$$

So we have found a solution of the equation (to about 10 decimal places).

Using solve for systems of equations: The solve command can also be used for solving several simultaneous equations for several unknowns. The most important thing to remember when dealing with systems is that the basic syntax of the `solve` statement `solve(what,how);` does not change -- since the "what" is now a collection of equations, and the "how" is a set of variables to solve for, some grouping symbols must be used so that Maple will know where the equations stop and the variables start. Maple syntax uses braces { } for this purpose. For example, the following statement solves a pair of linear equations for their unknowns:

```
> solve({3*x+2*y=5, x-4*y=7}, {x,y});
```

$$\left\{ y = \frac{-8}{7}, x = \frac{17}{7} \right\} \tag{12}$$

Within the braces, the equations and variables must be separated by commas.

As when one solves a single equation, the equations in a system can be referred to by name -- each equation can have its own name, or the whole collection can have one name:

```
> eqn1:=x+y=2:    eqn2:=x-y=2:
> solve({eqn1,eqn2},{x,y});
```

$$\{ y = 0, x = 2 \} \tag{13}$$

```
> eqns:=x^2-y^2=9,  x^2+y^2=41;
```

$$eqns := x^2 - y^2 = 9, x^2 + y^2 = 41 \tag{14}$$

```
> q:=solve({eqns},{x,y});
```

$$q := \{ x = 5, y = 4 \}, \{ x = -5, y = 4 \}, \{ y = -4, x = 5 \}, \{ x = -5, y = -4 \} \tag{15}$$

In this last statement, we have assigned the result to the variable `q` -- recall again that `solve` just tells you what the answer is (if it can), it does not change the values of any variables. In this example, `q` is now a list of four sets ..`q[1]` is the first set etc. up to `q[4]`. It is possible to use these sets in conjunction with the `subs` command, as in

```
> subs(q[2],x+y);
```

$$-1 \tag{16}$$

This statement substituted the second solution (`y=4` and `x=-5`) into the expression `x+y`.

The same considerations given above about solving one equation apply to systems.

Sometimes, the result will contain special functions from advanced mathematics which may be unfamiliar to you. And sometimes solve will not report any solution, either because there is none or because it is impossible to express the solution precisely in "closed form". The fsolve and evalf commands may be used in this context just as in the single variable context.

Hints, errors, special cases...

1. When working with systems of equations, it is usually a good idea to assign a name to the set of equations you want to solve. This makes your work easier to read. (It also helps avoid the most common syntax error when solve -ing systems of equations, which is to forget the braces around the list of equations). Example:

```
> c:='c';
> eqns:={a*x+b*y=c,d*x+e*y=f};
```

$$c := c \tag{17}$$

$$eqns := \{ax + by = c, dx + ey = f\}$$

```
> solve(eqns,{x,y});
```

$$\left\{ x = -\frac{-ec+fb}{-db+ae}, y = \frac{-dc+af}{-db+ae} \right\} \tag{18}$$

This is also an example where there are many variable names, but we solved for two, because we had two equations.

2. Shortcut #1: If (one of) your equation(s) is of the form "expression=0", it is not necessary to include the "=0" part -- Maple will assume that you intend to set any loose expression equal to zero. Example:

```
> solve(x^2-5*x,x);
```

$$0, 5 \tag{19}$$

3. Shortcut #2: If you are solving n equations (n can be any number at least 1), and there are precisely n variables used in the equations, it is not necessary to specify the variable list (the "how" part) -- Maple will assume that you want to solve for all the variables that are there. Example:

```
> solve({x+2=y,x+y=2});
```

$$\{x=0, y=2\} \tag{20}$$

4. It is possible that the number of equations and the number of unknowns can be different. If there are more equations than unknowns, then it is quite likely that there will be no solutions to the system of equations. On the other hand, if there are more unknowns than equations, then it is likely that some of the unknowns will be "free" in the solution -- this means that their values can be specified arbitrarily and the other variables solved for in terms of these. Examples:

```
> solve(x+y=2,x);
```

$$2 - y \tag{21}$$

```
> solve(x+y=2,{x,y});
```

$$\{x=2-y, y=y\} \tag{22}$$

In this last output, the equation "y=y" is how Maple indicates that y is a "free" variable, and x is defined in terms of it.

5. It is possible to use the solve command to solve inequalities as well as equations. Example:

```
> solve(x^2+2*x<5);
```

$$RealRange(Open(-1-\sqrt{6}), Open(-1+\sqrt{6})) \tag{23}$$

You can even combine equations and inequalities:

```
> sys:={x^2+y^2<4,x+y=2}:
> solve(sys,{x,y});
```

$$\{x=2-y, 0 < y, y < 2\} \tag{24}$$

6. (Advanced, obscure topic) Solve can also be used to find functions which are defined algebraically in terms of other functions:

```
> solve(f(x)^2+2*x=-1,f);
```

$$\mathbf{proc}(x)\ \mathrm{RootOf}(\_Z{^\wedge}2 + 2*x + 1, \mathit{label}{=}\_L1)\ \mathbf{end\ proc} \tag{25}$$

Note that the solution(s) are given in the long "proc" form of function definition.

7. The most common error to make when using solve (other than syntax errors) is to have inadvertently given the variable a value in previous work:

```
> x:=5:
> solve(x+4=8,x);
Error, (in solve) a constant is invalid as a variable, 5
```

8. Online help for solve can be found in the Help Contents browser using the path Mathematics -> Finding Roots -> solve.

fsolve

Use `fsolve` to have Maple use numerical approximation techniques (as opposed to algebraic methods used by **solve**) to find a decimal approximation to a solution of an equation or system of equations.

The syntax of `fsolve` is the standard Maple syntax:

`fsolve(what,how) ;`

where "what" stands for the equation (or system of equations) to be solved and "how" refers to the variable(s) being solved for.

To read more about setting up equations for solution, see the description of the `solve` command.

Using *fsolve* to solve a single equation: Because `fsolve` uses numerical techniques rather than algebraic ones, it is required that the number of equations be precisely the same as the number of variables being solved for. So, when fsolving one equation, it is crucial that there be exactly one unspecified variable in the equation.

There are two ways to use the `fsolve` command. The first is precisely like the `solve` command:

```
> restart;
> fsolve(x^2+5*x=17,x);
```
$$-7.321825380, 2.321825380 \tag{1}$$

This demonstrates that `fsolve`, like `solve`, knows how many roots to expect of a polynomial and will attempt to find them all (even if some are complex). When solving a transcendental equation, `fsolve` is usually content to find one solution.

The second way to use `fsolve` is especially important when an equation has many solutions, and you want to pick out a specific one. In this version of `fsolve`, it is possible to specify a domain (interval) in which the solution should be found. For example, consider the equation

```
> eqn:=x=tan(x);
```

$$eqn := x = \tan(x) \tag{2}$$

As we can see from plotting both sides, this equation has many solutions:

```
> plot({x,tan(x)},x=-8..8,-8..8,discont=true,thickness=
  2,color=black);
```

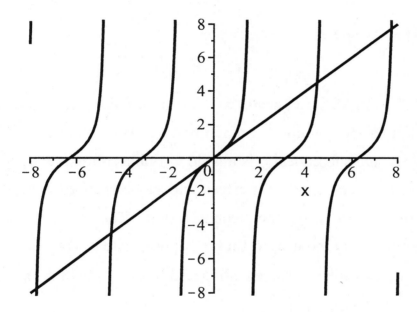

Just using fsolve on this equation will find one solution:

```
> fsolve(eqn,x);
```

$$0. \tag{3}$$

Now, suppose we want to find the solution between 6 and 8. Then we enter:

```
> fsolve(eqn,x,x=6..8);
```

$$7.725251837 \tag{4}$$

```
> tan(%);
```

$$7.725251841 \tag{5}$$

So we have found the solution to about 7 decimal places.

What can go wrong? Aside from syntax errors, there are a few things that can go wrong when using `fsolve`. First, as with solve, it is possible that the "variable" in the equation to be solved has already been given a value (perhaps one that was forgotten in the course of the Maple session). This results in the following response:

```
> x:=3: fsolve(x^2=4,x);
Error, (in fsolve) invalid arguments
```

The other things that can go wrong involve Maple's seeming inability to find a solution. This can result from one of two situations: first, there might be no solution -- second, the numerical procedure being used by Maple might need a little assistance from the user. For example:

```
> x:='x':fsolve(sin(x)=exp(x^2),x);
```

$$fsolve\left(\sin(x) = e^{\left(x^2\right)}, x\right) \tag{6}$$

This "non-response" from Maple indicates that it cannot find a solution. But that is because this equation has no solutions. Sometimes, `fsolve` chooses its initial approximation poorly and subsequently is unable to find a solution even if it exists. In this case Maple returns a message to this effect, and suggests choosing a "different" starting interval. In this case, using the second version of `fsolve` with specified domain will remedy the problem. (Of course, to find the appropriate domain the most reasonable thing to do is plot the two sides of the equation and look for the intersection point!).

Finally , `fsolve` will return an error message if there is a different number of equations than unknowns:

```
> fsolve(a*x=1,x);
Error, (in fsolve) a is in the equation, and is not
solved for
```

Of course, the `solve` command is able to handle this equation easily.

```
> solve(a*x=1,x);
```

$$\frac{1}{a} \tag{7}$$

Using `fsolve` to solve systems of equations: To be consistent with its "what","how" syntax, `fsolve` requires that a system of equations be enclosed in braces { } and that the list of variables being solved for also be so enclosed. For example:

```
>  fsolve({2*x+y=17,x^2-y^2=20},{x,y});
```

$$\{x = 16.37758198, y = -15.75516397\} \tag{8}$$

It is important to remember that the number of equations must be the same as the number of unknowns, and that no other (unspecified) variables are allowed in the equations:

```
>  fsolve({a*x+y=13,b*x-y=20},{x,y});
Error, (in fsolve) {a, b} are in the equation, and are
not solved for
```

Finally, we note that it is possible (and often advisable) to give `fsolve` a domain to search in -- this is done by giving an interval for each variable separately, thereby providing fsolve with a rectangular box-like region in which to find a solution. For example, let's consider the system solved above:

```
>  eqn1:=2*x+y=17:  eqn2:=x^2-y^2=20:
```

We give the equations names mostly to remind you that this is possible. Experimenting with several plots ultimately resulted in the following, which shows that our "`fsolve`" statement above returned only one of the two intersection points (the point in the 4th quadrant):

```
>  plot({17-2*x,sqrt(x^2-20),-sqrt(x^2-20)},x=4..20,
   color=black,thickness=2);
```

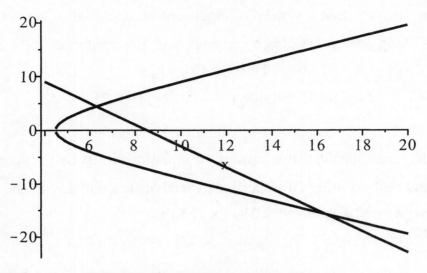

We can force **fsolve** to find the leftmost one as follows:

```
> fsolve({eqn1,eqn2},{x,y},{x=4..8,y=0..10});
```

$$\{x = 6.289084683, y = 4.421830634\} \qquad \textbf{(9)}$$

The syntax here is important! First comes the set of equations to solve (enclosed in braces), then the set of variables to solve for (enclosed in braces) and then the list of ranges for the variables (enclosed in braces). Only the third of these (the list of variable ranges) is optional when solving systems of equations. The other two must be present.

As usual with **solve** and **fsolve**, we can substitute this solution (just as it is!) back into the equations to make sure it is correct. First, we give it a name:

```
> s:=%;
```

$$s := \{x = 6.289084683, y = 4.421830634\} \qquad \textbf{(10)}$$

```
> subs(s,eqn1),subs(s,eqn2);
```

$$17.00000000 = 17, \ 19.99999999 = 20 \qquad \textbf{(11)}$$

So it seems to work. One final note -- when you give intervals for the variables, it is necessary to give them for *all* of the variables. **fsolve** will return nothing if intervals are specified for some but not all variables.

plot (basic plotting)

The `plot` command is probably the command you will use most often in Maple. The purpose of this command, of course, is to produce (two-dimensional) plots.

The syntax of the `plot` command in general follows the basic Maple

```
plot(what,how);
```

pattern, but both the "what" and the "how" can get pretty complicated.

In the most basic form of the `plot` statement, "what" is an expression to be plotted and "how" indicates the domain on the horizontal axis over which the plot is to be displayed:

```
> restart:
> plot(x^2-x,x=-2..2);
```

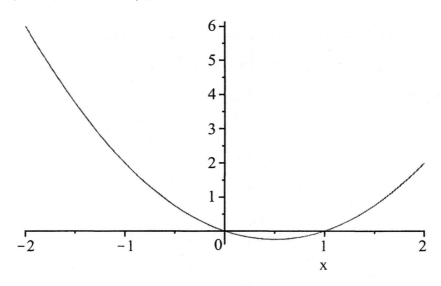

Notice here that Maple automatically chose a scale on the vertical axis. The scale it chooses is such that the plot over the entire specified domain is visible (i.e., the graph does not "run off" the top of the plot). It is possible to restrict the range on the vertical axis as well, as follows:

```
> plot(x^2-x,x=-2..2,y=-1..2);
```

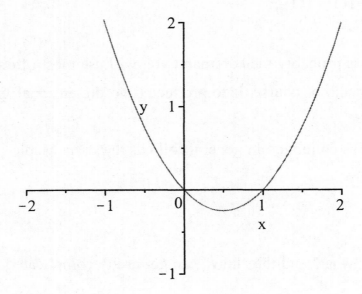

There is another important difference between the two plots above besides the change of scale on the vertical axis -- namely, the vertical axis on the second plot has a label. Maple takes the axis labels from the left side of the domain and range specifications.

It is possible not to give the label for the vertical axis, if you don't want it printed. If the "what" to plot is an expression, the variable in the domain specification must be specified, however. This is illustrated by the following:

```
> plot(x^2-x,x=-2..2,-1..2);
```

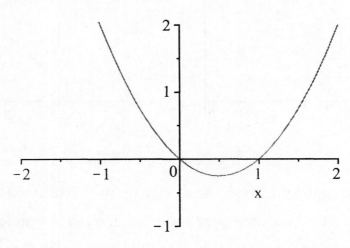

Plotting more than one curve on the same axes: It is possible to do this. But Maple looks for the first (un-parenthesized) comma in the `plot` syntax to dilineate the "what" from the "how". Thus, your list of things to plot must be enclosed within braces `{ }`. For example:

```
> plot({x^2,x^3},x=-2..2,y=-2..2,color=black);
```

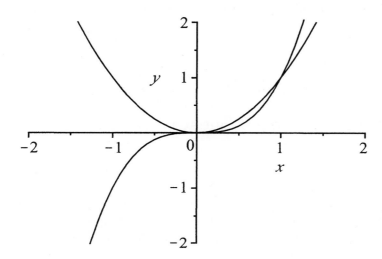

Common errors in basic plotting: The most common syntax error to make while plotting is to forget the braces when you are plotting more than one curve on the same axes. Other than syntax errors, the most common mistakes to make when plotting involve incorrect specification of variables. There are two kinds of errors:

1. <u>Using a domain value that already has a specific value</u>: It is important to make sure that the variable that is supposed to vary during the plot isn't already declared to be a constant (perhaps in the distant past during the Maple session). Making this error results in an error message, because Maple thinks you are trying to assign a new value to a constant ("invalid arguments"):

```
> x:=3:
> plot(x^2,x=-2..2);
Error, (in plot) invalid arguments
```

(Now we reset the value of x so that we don't run into the problem we have just illustrated.)

```
> x:='x';
```

$$x := x \tag{1}$$

2. <u>Not specifying a domain variable, or specifying the wrong domain variable</u> If your expression involves `t`, then you must let `t=-2..2`, not `x=-2..2` (or whatever the range is). This kind of mistake results in the dreaded "invalid arguments" or "empty plot" messages:

```
> plot(t^3,x=-2..2);
```

```
Warning, unable to evaluate the function to numeric
values in the region; see the plotting command's help
page to ensure the calling sequence is correct

Error, empty plot
> plot(t^3,-2..2);
```

```
Warning, unable to evaluate the function to numeric
values in the region; see the plotting command's help
page to ensure the calling sequence is correct

Error, empty plot
```

FANCIER PLOTTING:

The `plot` command is incredibly powerful and versatile. All of the ins and outs of plot options take a fair amount of getting used to. We will cover a few of them here.

Plotting points: It is possible to have Maple plot points. This is often useful when comparing empirical data with a mathematical model. There are two ways to do this, depending on how the points are generated. If you have a list of specific points to plot, you can assign them to a name as follows (you may replace the name "ptlst" with any of your own choosing -- except those in the list of "reserved words"):

```
> ptlst:=[1,2],[1.5,1],[2,-1],[2.5,0.5],[3,1],[3.5,0.6],
    [4,0.2]:
```

In this statement, the variable`ptlst` is a list of points. Each point is an ordered pair of numbers enclosed in square brackets (this is different from the usual convention in mathematics of using parentheses to enclose the coordinates in a point). To plot the list, we must enclose the entire list in square brackets, as follows:

> `plot([ptlst]);plot([ptlst],style=POINT);`

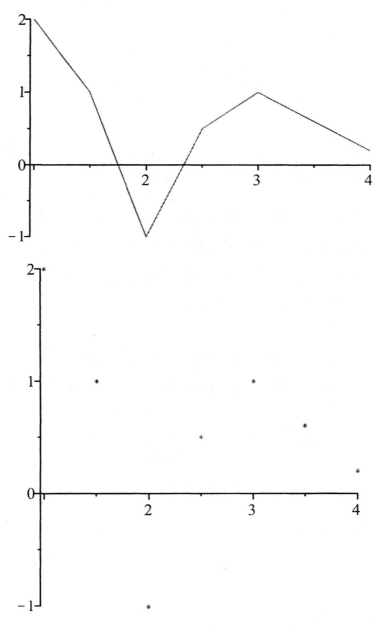

Note the difference between the plots--the first one is the default with line segments joining the points; the second plot (through the "style=point" option) plots only the points without connecting line segments. Maple can use other symbols for the points, including circles and boxes. The optional phrase: `symbol=circle` or `symbol=box` is used for this purpose, as follows:

```
> plot([ptlst],style=POINT,symbol=circle);
```

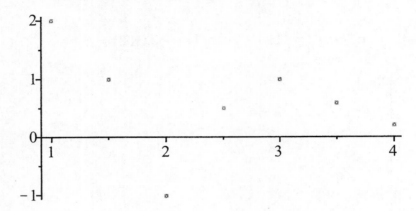

If you replace `style=POINT` with `style=LINE`, or if you don't specify a "style" (see the plot help page for more information) the dots will be connected by line segments (in the order the points were given -- this can make for interesting-looking and messy(!) plots if the points are not in ascending order of the absissa).

If the points come from evaluating an expression at several values of x, you can use `plot` in its usual form, but specify `style=POINT` (and a symbol option if you like):

```
> plot(x^2,x=-2..2,style=point,symbol=cross);
```

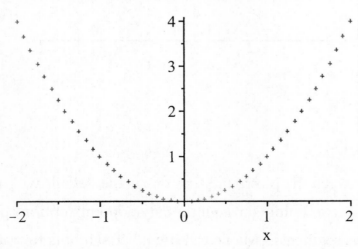

The minimum number of points plotted this way is about 50. You can insist that more points be plotted using the "numpoints" (number of points) option as follows:

```
> plot(x^2,x=-2..2,style=POINT,numpoints=150);
```

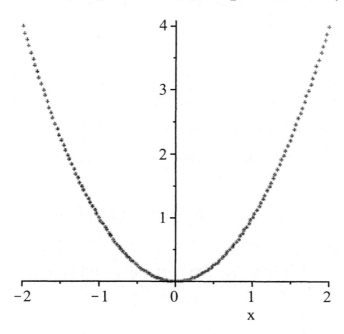

COMBINING PLOTS, Labelling Plots ...

Maple's fanciest specialty plotting functions are contained in a separate library called "`plots`". For basic plotting, there are two commands from the `plots` library which are especially useful: `textplot` and `display`. To load these two commands into your computer's memory, use the statement:

```
> with(plots,textplot,display);
```

$$[\textit{textplot, display}] \tag{2}$$

The `display` command is useful for combining different kinds of plots into one picture. The kinds of plots that can be combined are standard plots of expressions, plots of points, plots of text (what `textplot` is for, useful for labelling things), and animations.

For example, suppose we wish to combine the point plot of the variable "`ptlst`" we defined above, and a plot of the function `sin(3*x)`. To do this, we define two separate

69

plots, assign them to variables, and then display them together as follows:

```
> plot1:=plot([ptlst],style=POINT,symbol=circle):
> plot2:=plot(sin(3*x),x=0..4):
```

When defining and assigning plots, it is very advisable to use a colon rather than a semicolon. The thing that gets assigned to the variable (`plot1` and `plot2` in these examples) is Maple's list of internal instructions for producing the plot -- a long, complicated sequence of computer-speak that is best left undisplayed.

The display command uses the standard `display(what,how)` Maple syntax. In this case "what" is a set of "plot structures", and "how" is often an expression of the form `view=[a..b,c..d]`, which specifies the horizontal and vertical ranges to be displayed:

```
> display({plot1,plot2},view=[0..4,-1..2]);
```

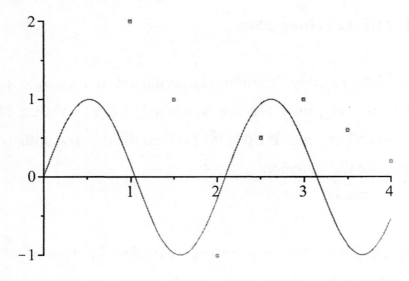

Another reason to use `display` is to attach labels to objects in your plots. You do this by putting the labels in a separate plot called a `textplot`. The `textplot` command takes as its argument a single or a set of "text objects", all of which look like `[a,b,`words`]` -- it places the words inside the quotes (they are both left quotes, on the keyboard to the left of the numeral 1) on the plot so that they are centered at the point (a, b). To see this at work, we plot a function and its derivative, and label them on a graph:

```
> y:=(1+x^2)*exp(-x^2/2): d:=diff(y,x):
> F:=plot({y,d},x=-3..3):
> G:=textplot({[1,1,`function`],[0.75,0.45,`derivative`]
    }):
> display({F,G});
```

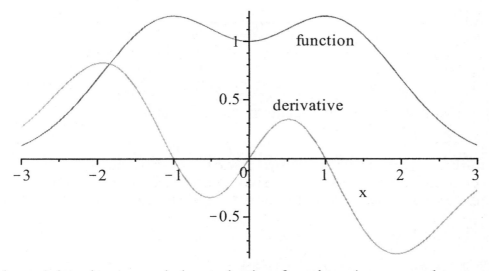

Optional special topic: A word about plotting functions (as opposed to expressions), and one situation in which it is a good idea: Sometimes, you will have the relationship you want to plot in the form of a function, rather than an expression, for example:

```
> f:=x->x^3*exp(-x):
```

In such a situation, you can simply plot f(x), which is an expression, using the information given above. Alternatively, you may use plot in the following form:

```
> plot(f,0..3);
```

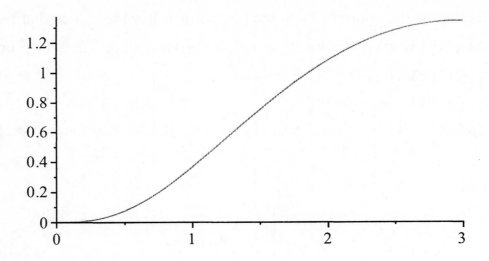

Usually, there is no particular reason to favor one version of `plot` over the other.

However, it is imperative not to confuse them. Neither statement

```
> plot(f(x),0..3);
```

```
Warning, unable to evaluate the function to numeric
values in the region; see the plotting command's help
page to ensure the calling sequence is correct
```

```
Error, empty plot
```

nor

```
> plot(f,x=0..3);
```

```
Error, (in plot) invalid plotting of procedures, perhaps
you mean plot(f, 0 .. 3)
```

will work correctly.

The one situation in which function-plotting is required is when you have defined a function that contains an "if-then" clause (a step-function, or piecewise-defined function). For example:

```
> f:=x-> if x<3 then x+1 else (x-1)^2 fi:
```

This function is equal to `x+1` if x is less than 3 and is equal to `(x-1)^2` otherwise. If we try to plot it ths usual way, we will get an error message:

```
> plot(f(x),x=0..5);
```

```
Error, (in f) cannot determine if this expression is
true or false: x < 3
```

This is because Maple attempts to understand the function before it has a value for x. On the other hand, the following way will work:

```
> plot(f,0..5);
```

(incidentally, from the plot we can see that f is probably continuous but not differentiable at x=3).

Plotting options: There are many options you can invoke when doing plots so that you can make the plot look like you want it. For example, you can control the color of a graph with the "color=" option (Maple knows many colors, for instance "color=red" or "color= green"), or make the curves plot thicker with the "thickness=" option (the plots above all use the default "thickness=1", but you can use bigger integers than 1 to get thicker plots). Another useful option is "scaling=constrained", which tells Maple to use the same scale on the x and y axes -- this makes circles look like circles rather than ellipses, and the slopes of lines are really what they appear to be. Here is a plot that uses all of these options:

```
> plot(x^2,x=-2..2,color=blue,thickness=3,scaling=
  constrained);
```

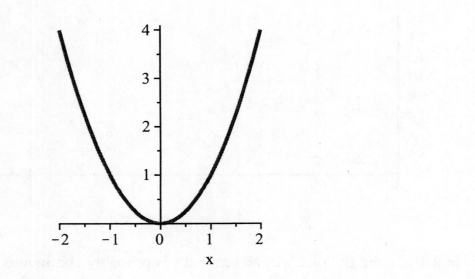

subs

The `subs` command is used to make substitutions of one expression (variable, number...) for another within some other (presumably more complicated) Maple expression. In other words, `subs` can be used for "plugging-in". The most important thing to remember about `subs` is that it merely reports what the result of making a substitution would be -- it does NOT change the value of any variable (unless the result of `subs` is assigned to a variable).

A few simple examples will give you the idea: Suppose
```
> restart;
> y:=x+3;
```
$$y := x + 3$$
Now you know that if you substitute 2 for x, y would be 5 -- to see this in Maple, type:
```
> subs(x=2,y);
```
$$5$$
Most importantly, after that statement it is still the case that:
```
> x;
```
$$x$$
i.e., x has no value (because it didn't before), and
```
> y;
```
$$x + 3$$
y is still what is was before.

The syntax of `subs` is the standard Maple:

```
subs(what,how);
```

syntax -- the "what" says what substitution (or set of substitutions) is to be made. The "how" is what expression to make the substitutions in. There is one deviation from standard Maple syntax -- if you have more than one substitution to make, it is not necessary (although it is permitted) to enclose the list of substitutions in braces. Thus, the following is a valid statement:

```
>  z:=x+sin(2*h):
>  subs(x=3*u+1,h=4*Pi*q,z);
```
$$3\,u + 1 + \sin\left(8\,\pi\,q\right)$$

Notice that the things being substituted can be quite complicated.

The thing being substituted for can also be complicated:

```
>  subs(sin(2*h)=4*w^2-1,z);
```
$$x + 4\,w^2 - 1$$

What to watch out for: Aside from syntax errors, there are few things that can go haywire when using `subs` - two stand out:

1. In certain situations, `subs` will not be able to find the expression you are substituing for if it is complicated (as in the last example) -- this has to do with the way Maple stores expressions internally. It is sometimes possible to "re-word" your substitution request so that Maple "gets it"- or else to break the task into several manageable ones.

2. You need not fear direct "circular substitutions" - for instance, using z from above:

```
>  z;
```
$$x + \sin\left(2\,h\right)$$

attempt the substitution:

```
>  subs(x=2*x,z);
```
$$2\,x + \sin\left(2\,h\right)$$

On the other hand, long chains of self-referential substitutions may produce unpredictable results. Could you have predicted the result of the following?

```
> subs(h=x,x=z,z);
```

$$x + \sin(2\,h) + \sin(2\,x + 2\,\sin(2\,h))$$

The following is different because substitutions in braces are made *simultaneously* instead of sequentially left-to-right:

```
> subs({h=x,x=z},z);
```

$$x + \sin(2\,h) + \sin(2\,x)$$

If things get too self-referential, Maple may generate a "stack overflow" message. The moral is that self-referential substitutions should be generally avoided, or done at most one at a time.

Why subs is useful: More often than not, it is better to use subs rather than to make assignments to the variables in an expression because subs reports the result of making a substitution without actually affecting the values of any variables. This leaves the definitions of the variables intact for later use.

For example, if

```
> y:=3*x^2+5*x+2;
```

$$y := 3\,x^2 + 5\,x + 2$$

and you want to compute the difference quotient (y(x+h)-y(x))/h, then you can write

```
> dq:=(subs(x=x+h,y)-y)/h;
```

$$dq := \frac{3\,(x+h)^2 + 5\,h - 3\,x^2}{h}$$

If x is undefined, we cannot set:

```
> x:=x+h;
```

```
Error, recursive assignment
```

since, as Maple is warning us, this assignment would make x be defined (circularly) in terms of itself. Hence, the assignment x:=x+h fails and x does not take on a new value.

```
>  x;
>  y;
```

$$x$$

$$3\,x^2 + 5\,x + 2$$

You could try just setting

```
>  x:=4;
```

$$x := 4$$

Then we can set

```
>  x:=x+h;
```

$$x := 4 + h$$

This just adds h to the old value of x and stores the result in x.
```
>  y;
```

$$3\,(4 + h)^2 + 22 + 5\,h$$

Or we could just set
```
>  x:=4;
```

$$x := 4$$

```
>  y;
```

$$70$$

That's fine, but now y is a number -- we can't plug any other values of x into it. So subs is a better way to do plugging-in.

A final note: The subs command is not what to use to do changes of variable in integrals (because it doesn't know about the dx part) - there is another Maple command, changevar in the student library, that is used for this purpose.

limit (and Limit)

The `limit` command is used to compute limits (what else?). The syntax of `limit` is Maple's usual

```
limit(what,how) ;
```

syntax. "What" in this case refers to "take the limit of what expression?", and "how" to "as what variable approaches what value?". For example, to compute

$$\lim_{x \to 2} \frac{3\,x - 6}{x^2 - 4}$$

we would enter:
```
> restart:
> limit((3*x-6)/(x^2-4),x=2);
```
$$\frac{3}{4}$$

Notice, the first argument of `limit` is the expression whose limit is being taken, and the second tells which variable approaches what number. If the limit does not exist, as in

```
> limit(1/x,x=0);
```

undefined

Maple tells you.

Occasionally, Maple will be unable to determine a limit (or whether it exists). In such a case, Maple will return nothing -- when this happens, you can give Maple an assist sometimes by setting a variable called "`Order`" equal to a whole number somewhat bigger than 6 (its default value) -- this works because Maple uses series to compute limits (you will see or have seen how to do this at the end of Math 104), and Maple usually uses only the first six terms of the series. When you change `Order`, you enable Maple to do more accurate (although more time-consuming) calculations. It is somewhat like computing to more decimal places.

The limits Maple takes are "two-sided, real limits". This means Maple assumes that when you type `x=15` as the second argument of limit, you mean x should approach 15 from either above or below through real values only (as opposed to complex ones). Maple can compute one-sided and complex limits. For example

```
> limit(1/x,x=0,right);
```

$$\infty$$

You could also do limits from the left.

It is possible to compute limits as x tends to infinity (or -infinity):

```
> limit(arctan(x),x=infinity);
```

$$\frac{1}{2}\pi$$

Finally, limits of functions of more than one variable are allowed:

```
> limit(x/(x^2+y^2),{x=0,y=0});
```

undefined

Remarks: It is always a good idea to use `plot` in conjunction with `limit` -- you can often get an intuition for the value of the limit from the plot.

It is instructive to use `limit` for computing derivatives and integrals from the definition.

Occasionally, to make your worksheets easier to read, you may wish to have Maple display a limit in standard mathematical notation without evaluating it. For this there is a capitalized, "inert" form of the limit command:

```
> Limit(exp(x)/(1-x),x=0);
```

$$\lim_{x \to 0} \frac{e^x}{1-x}$$

Sometimes, you can use the two forms together to produce meaningful sentences:

```
> Limit(exp(x)/(1-x),x=0)=limit(exp(x)/(1-x),x=0);
```

$$\lim_{x \to 0} \frac{e^x}{1-x} = 1$$

Few things can go wrong using the `limit` command, other than syntax errors -- except possibly that sometimes the variable in the `limit` command (the x above) has already been given a value that you forgot about:

```
> x:=3;
```

$$x := 3$$

```
> limit(x^2/sin(2*x^2),x=0);
Error, (in limit) invalid limiting point
```

80

Here, `limit` is objecting to your trying to let 3 approach 0.

diff (and Diff)

The `diff` command is used to compute derivatives of Maple expressions. The syntax of `diff` is Maple's usual

```
diff(what,how);
```

syntax. "What" in this case refers to "take the derivative of what?", and "how" to "with respect to what variable?". For example, to compute

$$\frac{\mathrm{d}}{\mathrm{d}x}\left(\frac{3\,x-6}{x^2-4}\right)$$

we would enter:

```
> restart:
> diff((3*x-6)/(x^2-4),x);
```

$$\frac{3}{x^2-4}-\frac{2\,(3\,x-6)\,x}{\left(x^2-4\right)^2} \tag{1}$$

Notice, the first argument of `diff` is the expression whose derivative is being taken, and the second tells with respect to what variable the derivative is being taken . This second part becomes crucial in expressions such as:

```
> diff(exp(a*x),x);
```

$$a\,\mathrm{e}^{ax} \tag{2}$$

where there are constants, parameters or other variables around. Maple assumes that you mean to take the derivative as the variable you specify changes, and that all other letters in the expression represent constants (but see the sections below on implicit differentiation and partial derivatives).

Maple can deal "theoretically" with derivatives of functions that do not yet have explicit definitions, For example, you may not have yet defined f(x) or g(x), but Maple can tell you that:

```
> diff(f(x)*g(x),x);
```

$$\left(\frac{d}{dx} f(x)\right) g(x) + f(x) \left(\frac{d}{dx} g(x)\right) \tag{3}$$

Notice that Maple uses the "rounded d" (partial derivative sign) for derivatives. This is a (reasonable) convention that was chosen by the people who produced the software.

Higher derivatives: There is a special notation for second, third, etc.. derivatives. Instead of typing:

```
> diff(diff(3*sin(x),x),x);
```

$$-3 \sin(x) \tag{4}$$

for the second derivative of 3sin(x), you may use either of the following (the second is easiest to type):

```
> diff(3*sin(x),x,x);
```

$$-3 \sin(x) \tag{5}$$

```
> diff(3*sin(x),x$2);
```

$$-3 \sin(x) \tag{6}$$

There are obvious extensions to this, using x$3, x$4, etc..

Examples: Here are a few examples of standard uses of derivatives, which combine `diff` with other basic Maple commands:

1. Find the slope of the tangent line to the graph of y=3*x/(x-2) at the point (x=3, y=9).
Solution: First define the variable y to be equal to the expression:

```
> y:=3*x/(x-2);
```

$$y := \frac{3x}{x-2} \tag{7}$$

Then take the derivative (we choose the name dy for the derivative):

```
> dy:=diff(y,x);
```

$$dy := \frac{3}{x-2} - \frac{3\,x}{(x-2)^2} \qquad \textbf{(8)}$$

Then substitute x=3 into the expression for the derivative of y:

```
> subs(x=3,dy);
```

$$-6 \qquad \textbf{(9)}$$

The slope at that point is -6. We can use this information to plot the graph of y together with its tangent line at (x=3,y=9) as follows:

```
> tangentline:=9-6*(x-3);
```

$$tangentline := 27 - 6\,x \qquad \textbf{(10)}$$

```
> plot([y,tangentline],x=2.5..4,color=[green,red],
  thickness=2);
```

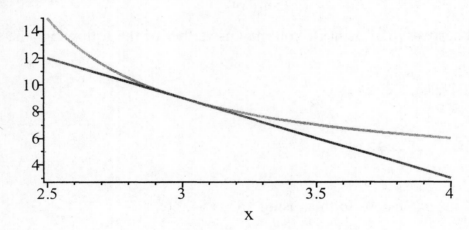

2. Find the maximum and minimum of the function `x*exp(-x)` on the (closed) interval `x=0..3`.

Solution: Since we are using Maple, we plot first and calculate later:

```
> y:=x*exp(-x);
```

$$y := x\,e^{-x} \qquad \textbf{(11)}$$

```
> plot(y,x=0..3,color=blue,thickness=2);
```

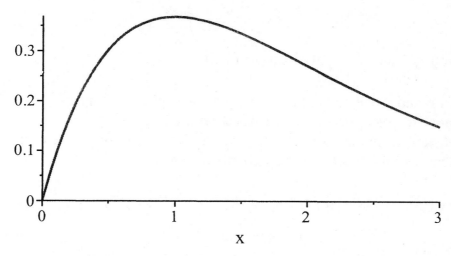

It looks like the minimum of y is zero (at x=0) and the maximum occurs for x=1 (which would make it 1/e). To verify this, we do the calculations. First we need to find the critical points of y (i.e., take the derivative and set it equal to zero):

```
> dy:=diff(y,x);
```

$$dy := e^{-x} - x\,e^{-x} \tag{12}$$

```
> solve(dy=0,x);
```

$$1 \tag{13}$$

This verifies our earlier observation that there is one critical point in the interval, at x=1. Now, we need to evaluate y at the critical point, and at the endpoints of the interval:

```
> subs(x=0,y), subs(x=1,y), subs(x=3,y);
```

$$0, e^{-1}, 3\,e^{-3} \tag{14}$$

We know which is the biggest and which is smallest from the plot, but it doesn't hurt to verify this numerically:

```
> evalf(%);
```

$$0., 0.3678794412, 0.1493612051 \tag{15}$$

To summarize, the maximum value of y is 1/e, which occurs when x=1, and the minimum is 0 which occurs when x=0.

Implicit differentiation: Maple knows how to take the derivative of both sides of an equation. As illustrated above (with the product rule), Maple can also "theoretically" take derivatives of functions whose definitions are not specified. What must be specified explicitly is the dependence of the function on its variable (This means that if you are thinking of y as being a function of x, you must write "y(x)" in your equations rather than

85

just "y").

Here is a typical implicit differentiation problem:

3. The variables x and y are related by the equation $x^2 y(x) - 3 y(x)^3 x = 0$. Find the slope of the graph of this equation at the point where x=3 and y=1.
Solution: First, define the equation, where we are considering y as a function of x (i.e., x is the independent variable and y is the dependent one):
```
> restart;
```
```
> eq:=x^2*y(x) - 3*y(x)^3*x = 0;
```

$$eq := x^2 y(x) - 3 y(x)^3 x = 0 \tag{16}$$

It is crucial to write y(x) everywhere. Now, we can take the derivative of both sides:

```
> deq:=diff(eq,x);
```

$$deq := 2 x y(x) + x^2 \left(\frac{d}{dx} y(x) \right) - 9 y(x)^2 x \left(\frac{d}{dx} y(x) \right) - 3 y(x)^3 = 0 \tag{17}$$

This gives the relationship among x, y and the derivative of y with respect to x. To solve the problem, we need to solve this equation for the derivative of y and then substitute x=3 and y=1 into the solution:

```
> solve(deq,diff(y(x),x));
```

$$-\frac{y(x)\left(2x - 3y(x)^2\right)}{x\left(x - 9y(x)^2\right)} \tag{18}$$

```
> subs(y(x)=1,x=3,%);
```

$$\frac{1}{6} \tag{19}$$

(Note: The order in which we did things, i.e., solve then substitute, is important, because substitution into the differentiated equation deq will replace pieces of the expression diff(y(x),x) with numbers -- which would be premature. Try it to see what goes wrong. You might also see what goes wrong if you replace the substitution statement above with "subs(x=3,y(x)=1,%);". This is a very good example which shows that substitutions are done from left to right.)

There is another way to do implicit differentiation by using the command "implicitdiff". Its syntax is:

```
> implicitdiff(f,y,x);
```

where **f** is the expression that you want to differentiate, **y** the dependent variable, and **x** the independent variable.

For example:
```
> implicitdiff(x^2*y-3*y^3*x=0,y,x);
```

$$ -\frac{y\left(2\,x-3\,y^2\right)}{x\left(x-9\,y^2\right)} \tag{20}$$

```
> subs(y=1,x=3,%);
```

$$ \frac{1}{6} \tag{21}$$

For more help on implicitdiff, type
```
> ?implicitdiff
```
and press the Return or Enter key to bring up the Help page for implicitdiff

Remarks: Occasionally, to make your worksheets easier to read, you may wish to have Maple display a derivative in standard mathematical notation without evaluating it. For this there is a capitalized, "inert" form of the `diff` command:
```
> Diff(exp(x)/(1-x),x);
```

$$ \frac{d}{dx}\left(\frac{e^x}{1-x}\right) \tag{22}$$

Sometimes, you can use the two forms together to produce meaningful sentences:
```
> Diff(exp(x)/(1-x),x)=diff(exp(x)/(1-x),x);
```

$$ \frac{d}{dx}\left(\frac{e^x}{1-x}\right) = \frac{e^x}{1-x} + \frac{e^x}{\left(1-x\right)^2} \tag{23}$$

Partial derivatives: Toward the middle of Math 114 and 115, you will learn how to take "partial derivatives" of functions of several variables. Maple can take partial derivatives as well as ordinary ones -- the same `diff` command is used for this. It is here that the "how" part of the `diff` command is especially important.

For example, here is a function of two variables x and y:

```
> f:=x^3*exp(y)-sin(x*y);
```

$$f := x^3 e^y - \sin(xy) \tag{24}$$

To take the partial derivative of f with respect to x, we use the command (notice the use of the capitalized form of the diff command):

```
> Diff(f,x)=diff(f,x);
```

$$\frac{\partial}{\partial x}\left(x^3 e^y - \sin(xy)\right) = 3 x^2 e^y - \cos(xy)\, y \tag{25}$$

For the partial derivative with respect to y, we would use:

```
> Diff(f,y)=diff(f,y);
```

$$\frac{\partial}{\partial y}\left(x^3 e^y - \sin(xy)\right) = x^3 e^y - \cos(xy)\, x \tag{26}$$

To take higher-order partial derivatives, we simply list the sequence of variables with respect to which to take the derivative:

```
> Diff(f,x,x,y)=diff(f,x,x,y);
```

$$\frac{\partial^3}{\partial y\, \partial x^2}\left(x^3 e^y - \sin(xy)\right) = 6 x e^y + \cos(xy)\, xy^2 + 2\sin(xy)\, y \tag{27}$$

Few things can go wrong using the diff command, other than syntax errors -- except possibly that sometimes the variable in the command (the x in "diff(... ,x) ") has already been given a value that you forgot about:

```
> x:=3;
```

$$x := 3 \tag{28}$$

```
> diff(x^2/sin(2*x^2),x);
Error, wrong number (or type) of parameters in function
diff
```

88

Here, `diff` is objecting to your trying to take the derivative "with respect to 3".

Another common error is to forget the "how" (x) part entirely: For instance

```
> diff(3*t^5);
Error, wrong number (or type) of parameters in function
diff
```

instead of

```
> diff(3*t^5,t);
```

$$15\,t^4 \tag{29}$$

int (and Int)

The `int` command is used to compute both definite and indefinite integrals of Maple expressions. The syntax of `int` is Maple's usual

```
int(what, how ) ;
```

syntax. "What" in this case refers to "take the integral of what?", and "how" to "with respect to what variable?" (and also "over what interval?" if the integral is a definite one). For example, to compute

$$\int \frac{3x - 6}{x^2 - 4}\, dx$$

we would enter:
```
> restart:
> int((3*x-6)/(x^2-4),x);
```

$$3 \ln(x + 2) \tag{1}$$

Notice, the first argument of **int** is the expression whose integral is being taken, and the second tells with respect to what variable the integral is being done. In this example of an indefinite integral, notice that Maple does not provide a constant of integration. You will occasionally have to take this into account and provide your own constant.

The second "how" argument of **int** becomes crucial in expressions such as:
```
> int(exp(a*x),x);
```

$$\frac{e^{ax}}{a} \tag{2}$$

where there are constants, parameters or other variables around. Maple assumes that you mean to take the integral as the variable you specify changes, and that all other letters in the expression represent constants.

To compute a definite integral, you provide a "range" for the variable, just as in plot statements. For example, to compute:

$$\int_0^2 x^2 e^x \, dx \tag{3}$$

we enter
```
> int(x^2*exp(x),x=0..2);
```

$$2 e^2 - 2 \tag{4}$$

There are a few things that can go "wrong" when you use a computer algebra package to calculate integrals:

(1) The integral might be impossible to evaluate in closed form. When Maple encounters such an integral (or one it can't do for some other reason) it simply returns the "unevaluated" integral. For example:

```
> int(ln(sin(sqrt(x^12-5*x^7+50*x+2))),x);
```

$$\int \ln\left(\sin\left(\sqrt{x^{12} - 5\,x^7 + 50\,x + 2}\right)\right) dx \tag{5}$$

This indicates that Maple has "given up" on the integral (see the section below on numerical evaluation of integrals).

(2) The integral cannot be evaluated in closed form in terms of "elementary" functions (trig, exponential, powers, roots, logs), but mathematicians have assigned a special name to it (or a closely related integral) because it comes up a lot in applications. For example:

```
> int(sin(2*x)/x,x);
```

$$\mathrm{Si}(2\,x) \tag{6}$$

Here "Si" is the name of one of these "special functions of mathematical physics". To learn about such a function, if it comes up, use Maple's help facility. Typing

```
> ?Si
```

will bring up a window with somewhat helpful information about the "Si" function (at least its definition). You can be fairly (but not completely) certain that if Maple produces an answer in terms of one of these exotic functions then there is not an answer in terms of elementary functions.

(3) Doing the integral involves some hypotheses on the variables involved (ranges not specified for indefinite integrals), or there are complex (as in complex numbers) versions of the answers that may seem unfamiliar -- the telltale sign of this is an answer involving capital "I" (which Maple uses for the complex number $\sqrt{-1}$).
An example:

```
>  int(x^2*sqrt(1-sin(x)^2),x);
```

$$-\frac{\frac{1}{2} I \left(2 + 2 I x - x^2 - 2 e^{2 I x} + 2 I e^{2 I x} x + x^2 e^{2 I x} \right)}{\sqrt{e^{2 I x}}} \qquad (7)$$

Of course, this example is somewhat contrived, since if we used the obvious trig identity first, then Maple would have no problem:

```
>  int(x^2*cos(x),x);
```

$$x^2 \sin(x) - 2 \sin(x) + 2 x \cos(x) \qquad (8)$$

But this shows that it is sometimes wise to think a little before you press "enter".

Numerical integration: You can force Maple to apply a numerical approximation technique for definite integration (Maple uses techniques that are related to but more sophisticated than Simpson's rule and the trapezoidal rule) as follows:

```
>  evalf(Int(sqrt(1+x^10),x=0..1));
```

$$1.040899075 \qquad (9)$$

Notice that the `Int` command is capitalized in this statement -- this is to prevent Maple from attempting to evaluate the integral symbolically and then just "`evalf`"-ing the answer (see below for other uses of capitalized `Int`).

Multiple integrals (for Calculus II and beyond):

Maple can do "iterated" integrals once you have set them up. For example, to perform the double integration:

$$\int_2^3 \int_0^y x^2 y^3 \, dx \, dy \tag{10}$$

use the statement:

```
> int(int(x^2*y^3,x=0..y),y=2..3);
```

$$\frac{2059}{21} \tag{11}$$

Note that this is literally an iterated integral -- one int expression is nested inside another. The usual rules about limits (especially that the outer integral must have constant limits) apply.

Remarks: Occasionally, to make your worksheets easier to read, you may wish to have Maple display an integral in standard mathematical notation without evaluating it. For this there is a capitalized, "inert" form of the int command:

```
> Int(exp(x)/(1-x),x);
```

$$\int \frac{e^x}{1-x} \, dx \tag{12}$$

or, for a definite integral:

```
> Int(ln(1+3*x),x=1..4);
```

$$\int_1^4 \ln(1 + 3x) \, dx \tag{13}$$

Sometimes, you can use the two forms together to produce meaningful sentences:

```
> Int(ln(1+3*x),x=1..4)=int(ln(1+3*x),x=1..4);
```

$$\int_1^4 \ln(1 + 3x) \, dx = \frac{13}{3} \ln(13) - 3 - \frac{8}{3} \ln(2) \tag{14}$$

A few other things can go wrong using the int command, other than syntax errors -- for example, the variable in the command (the x above) has already been given a value that you forgot about:

```
>  x:=3;
```

$$x := 3 \qquad\qquad (15)$$

```
>  int(x^2/sin(2*x^2),x);
Error, (in int) wrong number (or type) of arguments
```

or

```
>  int(x^2/sin(2*x^2),x=0..3);
Error, (in int) wrong number (or type) of arguments
```

The other common mistake (especially with indefinite integrals) is to forget the "how" part (which is required):

```
>  int(y^2);
Error, (in int) wrong number (or type) of arguments
```

You must type:

```
>  int(y^2,y);
```

$$\frac{y^3}{3} \qquad\qquad (16)$$

dsolve

The basic Maple command for solving differential equations is "`dsolve`". The syntax of `dsolve` is the usual

```
dsolve(what,how);
```

syntax of most basic Maple commands. "What" refers to the differential equation (or system of differential equations) together with any initial conditions there might be -- if there is more than just one equation with no conditions, the ODEs must be enclosed in braces {}. The "How" part, like most solve routines in Maple, indicates the name of the variable or function for which a solution is desired.

It is useful to give names to all of the equations and initial conditions you are going to use in `dsolve` -- it makes the statements easier to read and can often save some typing. The dependent variable, usually y in the following examples, must be explicitly shown as a function of the independent variable, ususlly x, like this:
$y(x)$.
For example:
```
>  restart:
>  eq:=diff(y(x),x)=x*y(x);
```

$$eq := \frac{\mathrm{d}}{\mathrm{d}x} y(x) = x\, y(x) \tag{1}$$

```
>  init:=y(2)=1;
```

$$init := y(2) = 1 \tag{2}$$

Now, `eq` is the name of the differential equation we will solve, and `init` is the name of the initial condition. It is NECESSARY that we use `y(x)` rather than just `y` -- this indicates to Maple that we are thinking of `y` as the dependent variable and `x` as the independent one. To solve the equation WITHOUT the initial condition (i.e., to find the general solution), we

```
> dsolve(eq,y(x));
```

$$y(x) = \_C1\,e^{\frac{1}{2}x^2} \tag{3}$$

Notice the _C1 -- that is Maple's way of producing an "arbitrary constant". To solve the initial-value problem, we must group the equation and initial condition together in braces:

```
> dsolve({eq,init},y(x));
```

$$y(x) = \frac{e^{\frac{1}{2}x^2}}{e^2} \tag{4}$$

This last output is an equation -- if you wish to assign the output to a name, so that you can use it for further work (or to plot it, etc..) it is possible to use the "rhs" (right-hand side) command (and the percent sign, which refers to the last previous output):

```
> ans:=rhs(%);
```

$$ans := \frac{e^{\frac{1}{2}x^2}}{e^2} \tag{5}$$

More advanced uses of dsolve:

There are four additional ways to use dsolve for situations other than single first-order differential equations and initial-value problems.

1. **Equations of higher order.** Second (and higher) order equations can be solved with **dsolve**. To do this, recall that higher derivatives of a function are taken as follows in Maple (this is the third derivative of f(x)):

```
> diff(f(x),x$3);
```

$$\frac{d^3}{dx^3}f(x) \tag{6}$$

So, we can set up a second-order equation as follows:

```
> eqn2:=diff(y(x),x$2)+3*diff(y(x),x)+2*y(x)=exp(x);
```

$$eqn2 := \frac{d^2}{dx^2} y(x) + 3 \left(\frac{d}{dx} y(x) \right) + 2 y(x) = e^x \tag{7}$$

The general solution of this equation is:
```
> dsolve(eqn2,y(x));
```

$$y(x) = \frac{1}{6} e^x - e^{-2x} \_C1 + e^{-x} \_C2 \tag{8}$$

Notice that there are two constants, _C1 and _C2 (as is to be expected) in the solution. The appropriate initial-value problem requires two initial conditions -- one on the value of y at some value of x, and the other on the value of the derivative at that point. For this problem, we will specify value of y and its derivative [Maplese: D(y)(x)] at x=1:
```
> inits:=y(1)=2, D(y)(1)=4;
```

$$inits := y(1) = 2, \mathrm{D}(y)(1) = 4 \tag{9}$$

```
> dsolve({eqn2,inits},y(x));
```

$$y(x) = \frac{1}{6} e^x + \frac{1}{3} \frac{e^{-2x}(-18+e)}{e^{-2}} - \frac{1}{2} \frac{e^{-x}(-16+e)}{e^{-1}} \tag{10}$$

Sometimes these things get somewhat complicated!

2. **Systems of differential equations** In many applications, systems of differential equations arise. The syntax for these is the same as for initial-value problems (even when no initial values are specified) --- braces around the problem are required, AND braces around the list of functions to be solved for. We do one example of an initial value problem for a system of two first-order equations:

```
> eqns:=diff(y(x),x)+diff(z(x),x)=x, diff(y(x),x)-2*diff(z(x),x)=
  x^2;
```

$$eqns := \frac{d}{dx} y(x) + \frac{d}{dx} z(x) = x, \frac{d}{dx} y(x) - 2 \left(\frac{d}{dx} z(x) \right) = x^2 \tag{11}$$

```
> inits:= y(0)=1, z(0)=2;
```

$$inits := y(0) = 1, z(0) = 2 \tag{12}$$

```
> dsolve({eqns,inits},{y(x),z(x)});
```

$$\left\{ y(x) = \frac{1}{9} x^3 + \frac{1}{3} x^2 + 1, z(x) = -\frac{1}{9} x^3 + \frac{1}{6} x^2 + 2 \right\}$$ (13)

3. **Numerical solutions**: Very often, it is impossible to obtain the solution to a differential equation in closed form. In this case, one must resort to a numerical approximation method. Maple knows a lot of these -- to invoke them, use the `numeric` option of `dsolve`, as follows:

```
> eqn:=diff(y(x),x)+exp(y(x))*x^3=2*sin(x);  init:=y(0)=2;
```

$$eqn := \frac{d}{dx} y(x) + e^{y(x)} x^3 = 2 \sin(x)$$

$$init := y(0) = 2$$ (14)

```
> F:=dsolve({eqn,init},y(x),numeric);
```

$$F := \mathbf{proc}(x\_rkf45) \ ... \ \mathbf{end \ proc}$$ (15)

Your output for the preceeding statement might be slightly different. The output means that Maple has defined a function called F, that will output the value of y(x) corresponding to a given (numerical) value of x. For example:

```
> F(2);
```

$$[x = 2., y(x) = -0.7815971822233124910]$$ (16)

It is often useful to plot the numerically-obtained solution of a differential equation. To do this, you need to apply the Maple command `odeplot` to the result (F in this case) of the `dsolve(....,numeric)` statement. The `odeplot` command is in the `plots` library and so must be loaded using the statement:

```
> with(plots,odeplot);
```

$$[odeplot]$$ (17)

To plot the solution, use the following syntax:

```
> odeplot(F,[x,y(x)],-2..2,color=blue,thickness=2);
```

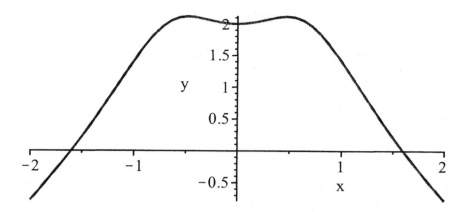

In this statement, the "F" is the function that resulted from dsolve(...numeric).
The second argument indicates to Maple which variables should be on which axis
(sometimes it is useful to plot x versus the derivative of y(x) or y(x) versus the derivative
of y(x)). The final argument gives the domain of the independent variable (x in this case)
over which the plot should be made.

The most important things to notice are:
 (a) You must assign the result of dsolve(......,numeric) to a NAME.
 (b) You must use the odeplot function from the plots library to plot the result of
dsolve(......,numeric) . The syntax is as above, and you can see some more
examples in Maple help.

4. **Series solutions**: You can also use dsolve to get power series solutions of
differential equations. It is usually best to specify an initial-value problem to do this. The
order to which the series is computed is determined by the system variable Order (just
as for the taylor command). For example, to solve the initial value problem y'+x*y=0,
y(0)=1 by series, you enter:
> dsolve({diff(y(x),x)+x*y(x)=0, y(0)=1},y(x), series);

$$y(x) = 1 - \frac{1}{2} x^2 + \frac{1}{8} x^4 + O(x^6) \tag{18}$$

If you want more terms:

```
> Order:=14: dsolve({diff(y(x),x)+x*y(x)=0, y(0)=1},y(x), series);
```

$$y(x) = 1 - \frac{1}{2}x^2 + \frac{1}{8}x^4 - \frac{1}{48}x^6 + \frac{1}{384}x^8 - \frac{1}{3840}x^{10} + \frac{1}{46080}x^{12} + O(x^{14}) \qquad (19)$$

```
> soln := rhs(convert(%, polynom))
```

$$soln := 1 - \frac{1}{2}x^2 + \frac{1}{8}x^4 - \frac{1}{48}x^6 + \frac{1}{384}x^8 - \frac{1}{3840}x^{10} + \frac{1}{46080}x^{12} \qquad (20)$$

The result of this operation is a Maple "series" (with the "big-O" term) which is then converted into a "polynomial" by the **convert** command so you can compute with it {see the discussion of this on the `taylor` help page (> ?taylor) for additional details}.

Errors:

The most common error one makes when using **dsolve** is to use the dependent variable (the "y" above) without specifying the dependence on the independent variable (in other words, using the y without writing $y(x)$). Unexpected results often happen when you do this.

The other kinds of errors are like the ones that go wrong whenever you use a solving or plotting routine -- e.g., the variables being solved for have already been assigned values (that may have been forgotten), etc..

DEtools (DEplot)

Maple's `DEtools` library contains several commands that are useful for plotting solutions of differential equations. We will use one of them to plot direction fields of first-order differential equations together with solution curves. The command is `DEplot`. Since it is in a library, we must first load it into memory by typing:

```
> with(DEtools,DEplot);
```

$$[\,DEplot\,]$$ **(1)**

The syntax of `DEplot` is *complicated*!!   The reason for this is that there is a lot of information you must supply to the program about the differential equation to be solved, initial conditions if solution curves are desired, and how to plot. The trick is to put it in the right order.

Example: Suppose we want to produce the direction field and some representative solution curves for the equation y'+x*y=1. And for some reason, we're interested in solutions defined near x=0, and y=0. We decide to have our plot window be for x from -2..2 and y from -2..2. We'll plot the direction field and some solution curves. Since the solutions are specified by their initial conditions, we plot the solutions corresponding to the conditions y(0)=-1, y(0)=-0.5, y(0)=0, y(0)=0.5 and y(0)=1. Here is the statement that does it all:

```
> DEplot(diff(y(x),x)=1-x*y(x),y(x),x=-2..2,{[0,-1],[0,-0.5],[0,
  0], [0,0.5],[0,1]}, y=-2..2,linecolor=black,color=black);
```

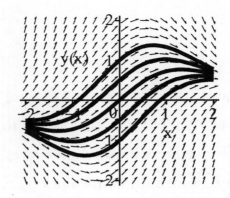

The pieces of the syntax are:

DEplot(...); -- the name of the command (obviously)

diff(y(x),x)=1-x*y(x) -- the differential equation. Note that the format of the differential equation is similar to that for dsolve. One difference, however, is that the diff(y(x),x) part of the differential equation must appear *by itself* on the left of the = sign -- that's why we subtracted the x*y(x) over to the right (otherwise the direction field is not plotted correctly).

y(x) -- tells the name of the dependent variable

x=-2..2 -- gives the range of values to be plotted on the x axis -- also the range of x values for which the solutions are to be computed.

{[0,-1],[0,-0.5],......} -- gives the initial conditions -- y(0)=-1 translates into going through the point [0,-1], etc.. Having too many of these can clutter the plot and can also take a long time to compute.

y=-2..2 -- gives the range of y to plot on the vertical axes (the solution curves are allowed to run off the plot).

That's basically it. There are only two minor variations:

1. If all you want is the direction field, without any sample solution curves, the initial conditions argument of DEplot may be omitted, as follows:

```
> DEplot(diff(y(x),x)=1-x*y(x),y(x),x=-2..2,y=-2..2,color=black);
```

2. Maple uses a numerical procedure to find the solution curves (Maple has been programmed with several, but a discussion of these is beyond the scope of this course). If the solutions look too "clunky" you can improve them by decreasing the stepsize " parameter (the "step size" is the spacing between values of the independent variable at which the solution is approximated; for example with a start value of $t = 0$, a stepsize $=1$ computes solutions at $t = 0$, 1, 2, 3, ... and a stepsize $=0.1$ computes solutions at $t = 0$, 0.1, 0.2, 0.3, ...);reducing the *stepsize* increases the accuracy and causes Maple to plot more points). But decreasing it too much can make the plot take a LONG time to produce without enough of an increase in accuracy--try a good course in numerical methods for the details. Here is an example with the stepsize parameter included (another example is found in the last example of this section; it illustrates what can happen if *stepsize* is too big):

```
> DEplot(diff(y(x),x)=x*y(x)^2,y(x),x=-1..1,{[0,0.5],[0,
  -0.5]},stepsize=0.05,y=-1..1,color=black,linecolor=
  black);
```

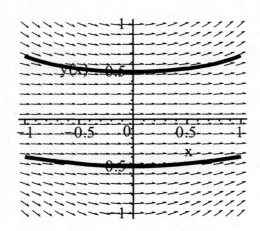

> ?DEplot

>

Unless the graph of the solutions looks "jagged", let Maple's stepsize programming work for you.

DEplot can be used to show solutions of systems of equations. The following is a Lotke-Volterra model of a preditor/prey system which models the variation in the population of a preditor and its prey as the two species interact This particular example is from the DEplot help pageNote the syntax in DEplot--first comes the system of equations enclosed in brackets as defined in the LVS:= <statement> below, then the list of functions for which a solution is desired (you can show individual solutiona by listing only $x(t)$ or $y(t)$ in the braces rather than both functions), ranges for the independent and dependent variables, and some plotting options (described on the DEplot help page):

> $LVS := \left[\dfrac{d}{dt} x(t) = x(t) \, (1 - y(t)), \dfrac{d}{dt} y(t) = 0.3 \, y(t) \, (x(t) - 1) \right]$

$$LVS := \left[\frac{d}{dt} x(t) = x(t) \, (1 - y(t)), \frac{d}{dt} y(t) = 0.3 \, y(t) \, (x(t) - 1) \right] \tag{2}$$

> $with(\ DEtools, DEplot) : DEplot(\ LVS, [\ x(t), y(t)\ ], t = 0\ ..10, x = -1\ ..2, y = -1$
$..2, arrows = large, title = \ `Lotka\text{-}Volterra\ model`, color = magnitude)$

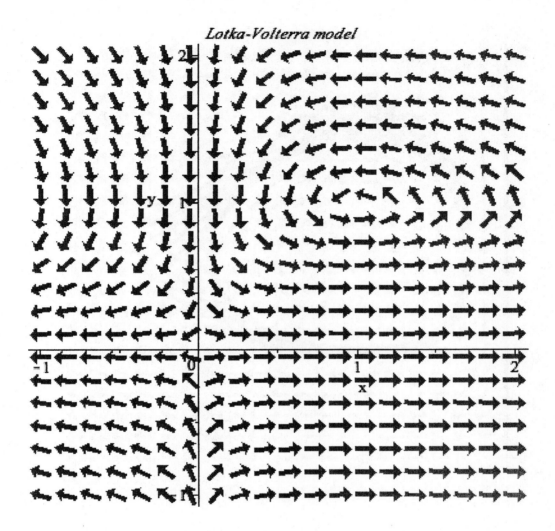

Lotka-Volterra model

Note that this version of DEplot produces only a slope field which easily allows you to visualize the population changes. The next example shows the particular solution for the initial conditions x(0)=1, y(0)=0.5:

```
>   DEplot( LVS, [ x( t ), y( t ) ], t = 0 ..100, x = 0 ..3, y = 0 ..2, arrows = large, [ [ x(0)
       = 1, y( 0 ) = 0.5] ], title= 'Lotka-Volterra model', linecolor = black)
```

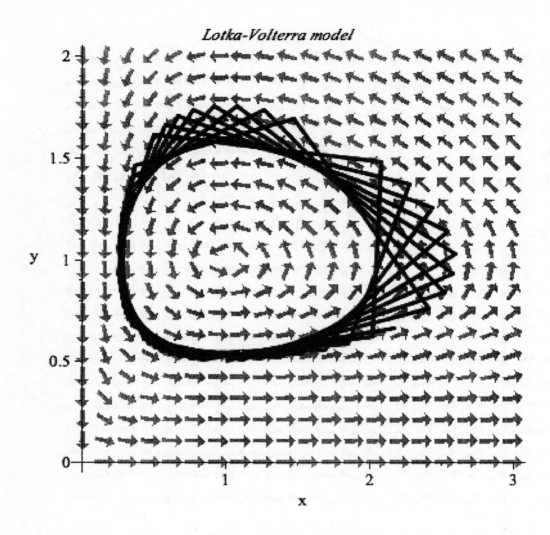

Lotka-Volterra model

Note the "jagged" appearance of parts of the solution curve--this occurred because the numerical solution routines were using too large a step size. A better representation can be obtained by using a smaller step size (experiment with a few to see at what step size gives a smooth curve--start with *stepsize=1* and decrease the stepsize by 0.1 each time until the solution is sufficiently smooth; in this example we will use*stepsize=0.05*:

> *DEplot(LVS, [x(t), y(t)], t=0..100, x=0..3, y=0..2, arrows=large, [[x(0) =1, y(0)=0.5]], stepsize=0.05, title=`Lotka-Volterra model`, linecolor =black)*

106

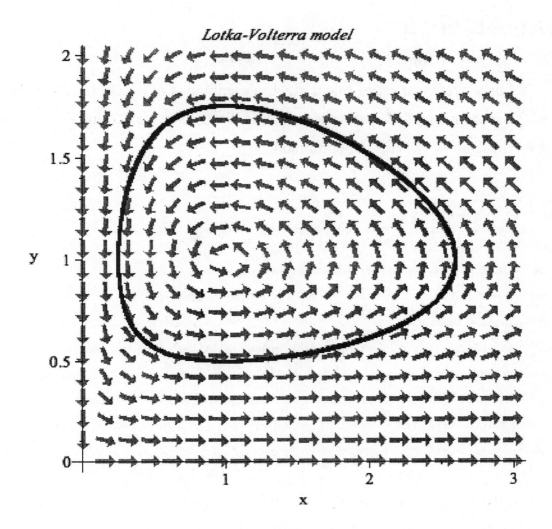

Linear Algebra

Maple has a fairly extensive set of linear algebra commands in two libraries: the older *linalg* and the more recent *LinearAlgebra* which is discussed here. To use *LinearAlgebra*, you must begin your work with the command:

```
> restart:
> with(LinearAlgebra)
Warning, inserted missing semicolon at end of statement
```

[*&x, Add, Adjoint, BackwardSubstitute, BandMatrix, Basis, BezoutMatrix, BidiagonalForm,* **(1)**

BilinearForm, CharacteristicMatrix, CharacteristicPolynomial, Column,

ColumnDimension, ColumnOperation, ColumnSpace, CompanionMatrix,

ConditionNumber, ConstantMatrix, ConstantVector, Copy, CreatePermutation,

CrossProduct, DeleteColumn, DeleteRow, Determinant, Diagonal, DiagonalMatrix,

Dimension, Dimensions, DotProduct, EigenConditionNumbers, Eigenvalues, Eigenvectors,

Equal, ForwardSubstitute, FrobeniusForm, GaussianElimination, GenerateEquations,

GenerateMatrix, Generic, GetResultDataType, GetResultShape, GivensRotationMatrix,

GramSchmidt, HankelMatrix, HermiteForm, HermitianTranspose, HessenbergForm,

HilbertMatrix, HouseholderMatrix, IdentityMatrix, IntersectionBasis, IsDefinite,

IsOrthogonal, IsSimilar, IsUnitary, JordanBlockMatrix, JordanForm, KroneckerProduct,

LA_Main, LUDecomposition, LeastSquares, LinearSolve, Map, Map2, MatrixAdd,

MatrixExponential, MatrixFunction, MatrixInverse, MatrixMatrixMultiply, MatrixNorm,

MatrixPower, MatrixScalarMultiply, MatrixVectorMultiply, MinimalPolynomial, Minor,

Modular, Multiply, NoUserValue, Norm, Normalize, NullSpace, OuterProductMatrix,

Permanent, Pivot, PopovForm, QRDecomposition, RandomMatrix, RandomVector, Rank,

RationalCanonicalForm, ReducedRowEchelonForm, Row, RowDimension, RowOperation,

RowSpace, ScalarMatrix, ScalarMultiply, ScalarVector, SchurForm, SingularValues,

SmithForm, StronglyConnectedBlocks, SubMatrix, SubVector, SumBasis, SylvesterMatrix,

ToeplitzMatrix, Trace, Transpose, TridiagonalForm, UnitVector, VandermondeMatrix,

VectorAdd, VectorAngle, VectorMatrixMultiply, VectorNorm, VectorScalarMultiply,

ZeroMatrix, ZeroVector, Zip]

The basic linear algebra operations you will need to use are :

a) Defining matrices (the "matrix" command and palette) and displaying them ("evalm")

b) Matrix multiplication (the "MatrixMatrixMultiply " and "MatrixVectorMultiply" commands and the "." and "&*" operators)

c) Row reduction commands ("Pivot" "LinearSolve" and "GaussianElimination ")

d) Inverse of a matrix using "MatrixInverse" or ^(-1) power

e) dot (inner) and cross products of vectors using "DotProduct" and "CrossProduct"

f) finding eigenvalues and eigenvectors and diagonalizing a matrix using "Eigenvalues" and "Eigenvectors"

Matrices are defined with the "matrix" command or the matrix palette (below). One way to make a matrix is to list its entries, each row being enclosed in brackets as follows:

```
>  M:=Matrix([[3,-1,2],[2,8,8],[3,1,1]]);
```

$$M := \begin{bmatrix} 3 & -1 & 2 \\ 2 & 8 & 8 \\ 3 & 1 & 1 \end{bmatrix} \qquad (2)$$

A useful alternative in Maple 12 is to use the Matrix Palette on the left side of the worksheet--open the pallette (click on the triangle to the left of the name), select the number of rows and columns and choose the type (usually the default "Custom values" is what you want, but you can choose among others such an identity matrix or random entries among others), shape (triangular, diagonal and many others) and data type (from among all of Maple's recognized types including floating point, various length integers and complex).

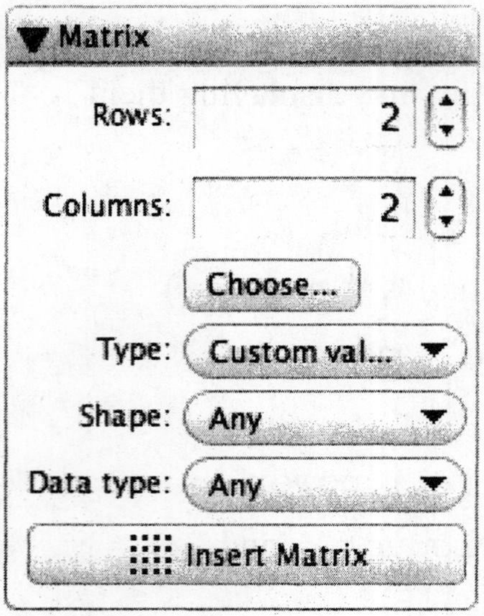

▼ Matrix

Rows: 2

Columns: 2

Choose...

Type: Custom val... ▼

Shape: Any ▼

Data type: Any ▼

▦ Insert Matrix

For instance, to enter a 2x2 matrix into which you can type values, you can use the setup shown above, type the matrix name and an assignment operator (:=), then press the "Inser Matrix" button. The result is a matrix with placeholders for the values with the 1, 1 position selected; to move between entries press the tab key:

$$> \quad myMatrix := \begin{bmatrix} m_{1,1} & m_{1,2} \\ m_{2,1} & m_{2,2} \end{bmatrix}$$

Now type in the desired values--the cursor moves along each row then to the nest row as you press the TAB key:

$$> \quad myMatrix := \begin{bmatrix} 2 & 4 \\ -5 & 1.1 \end{bmatrix}$$

$$myMatrix := \begin{bmatrix} 2 & 4 \\ -5 & 1.1 \end{bmatrix} \tag{3}$$

If you make a typing error defining a matrix, you can edit the original statement or change one entry at a time as follows <matrixName>[row #, column #] := <new value>; for example, to change the entry in the second row, first column of a matrix named myMatrix to 5:

```
> myMatrix[2,1]:=5;
```

$$myMatrix_{2,1} := 5 \tag{4}$$

110

This changes the entry in the second row, first column:

```
>  myMatrix;
```

$$\begin{bmatrix} 2 & 4 \\ 5 & 1.1 \end{bmatrix}$$

(5)

```
>  evalm(myMatrix);
```

$$\begin{bmatrix} 2 & 4 \\ 5 & 1.1 \end{bmatrix}$$

(6)

Note that in earlier versions of Maple, to see myMatrix, you **must** use evalm (for "evaluate as a matrix"); Maple 12 requires only the name of the matrix be typed.

Now let's try computing the dot and cross product of two vectors.

```
>  v1 :=
```
$\begin{bmatrix} 2 \\ 3 \\ 5 \end{bmatrix}$;

$$v1 := \begin{bmatrix} 2 \\ 3 \\ 5 \end{bmatrix}$$

(7)

```
>  v2 :=
```
$\begin{bmatrix} 9 \\ 5 \\ 1 \end{bmatrix}$

$$v2 := \begin{bmatrix} 9 \\ 5 \\ 1 \end{bmatrix}$$

(8)

```
>  DotProduct( v1, v2 ); CrossProduct ( v1, v2 )
```
$$38$$

$$\begin{bmatrix} -22 \\ 43 \\ -17 \end{bmatrix}$$

(9)

The dot product van also be computed as $v^T v$:

> *Transpose* $(v1).v1;$

38

(10)

Ordinary scalar operations can be performed as usual:

> $5 \cdot myMatrix, v1 + v2;$

$$\begin{bmatrix} 10. & 20. \\ 25. & 5.50000000000000000 \end{bmatrix}$$

$$\begin{bmatrix} 11 \\ 8 \\ 6 \end{bmatrix}$$

(11)

Solving Linear Systems

If we want to solve the system of equations:

$3x - y + 2z = 4$

$5x + 8y + 8z = 6$

$3x + y + z = -2$,

we need to build a matrix with the coefficients of the system of equations and do Gaussian elimination. The Maple commands are:

1) choose a name and use the matrix palette to insert a 3x4 matrix for the system, then fill in the coefficients:

> $S := \begin{bmatrix} 3 & -1 & 2 & 4 \\ 5 & 8 & 8 & 6 \\ 3 & 1 & 1 & -2 \end{bmatrix}$

$$S := \begin{bmatrix} 3 & -1 & 2 & 4 \\ 5 & 8 & 8 & 6 \\ 3 & 1 & 1 & -2 \end{bmatrix}$$

(12)

2) use `LinearSolve` to produce a solution from the augmented matrix S

> `LinearSolve(S);`

112

$$\begin{bmatrix} -\dfrac{22}{19} \\[2mm] -\dfrac{86}{57} \\[2mm] \dfrac{170}{57} \end{bmatrix} \qquad\qquad \textbf{(13)}$$

You can see that the solution of the system is: x= -22/19, y= -86/57 and z=170/57.

Using GaussianElimination produces aan echelon form but doesn't complete the solution as LinearSolve does:

> *GaussianElimination* (*S*);

$$\begin{bmatrix} 3 & -1 & 2 & 4 \\[2mm] 0 & \dfrac{29}{3} & \dfrac{14}{3} & -\dfrac{2}{3} \\[3mm] 0 & 0 & -\dfrac{57}{29} & -\dfrac{170}{29} \end{bmatrix} \qquad\qquad \textbf{(14)}$$

Alternatively, we can find the inverse of the coefficient matrix (M) and multiply it by the right hand side vector (Rs):

> *M* := $\begin{bmatrix} 3 & -1 & 2 \\ 5 & 8 & 8 \\ 3 & 1 & 1 \end{bmatrix}$

$$M := \begin{bmatrix} 3 & -1 & 2 \\ 5 & 8 & 8 \\ 3 & 1 & 1 \end{bmatrix} \qquad\qquad \textbf{(15)}$$

> *Rs* := $\begin{bmatrix} 4 \\ 6 \\ -2 \end{bmatrix}$

$$Rs := \begin{bmatrix} 4 \\ 6 \\ -2 \end{bmatrix} \qquad\qquad \textbf{(16)}$$

Now compute the inverse of M using the `MatrixInverse` command:

113

> $Minv := MatrixInverse(M);$

$$Minv := \begin{bmatrix} 0 & -\dfrac{1}{19} & \dfrac{8}{19} \\[2mm] -\dfrac{1}{3} & \dfrac{1}{19} & \dfrac{14}{57} \\[2mm] \dfrac{1}{3} & \dfrac{2}{19} & -\dfrac{29}{57} \end{bmatrix}$$ (17)

And produce the solution by multiplying the inverse matrix and right side vector using the "." operator (or use MatrixVectorMultiply):

> $Soln := Minv.Rs$

$$Soln := \begin{bmatrix} -\dfrac{22}{19} \\[2mm] -\dfrac{86}{57} \\[2mm] \dfrac{170}{57} \end{bmatrix}$$ (18)

Thus, the important commands for setting up and solving linear systems are:

1. `Matrix Palette` -- this is used to enter matrices -- note the choices you can make to customize the matrix as described above.

2. `evalm` -- to see a matrix, can either enter its name and press RETURN or you can use "`evalm`" -- occasionally, it will be necessary to `evalm` partial results of a matrix computation in order to use them again. The general rule is that you may use `evalm` anytime you use the name of a matrix, as in `evalm(A)`, `evalm(M)` etc.

3. `LinearSolve` -- use `augment` to create an augmented matrix, i.e., to put the extra column on the right side of a square matrix so that the result represents a system of equations. Note that you must use "`vector`" to make the right side into a vector, as shown above.

4. `GaussianElimination` -- performs gaussian row reduction on a matrix--useful

114

for checking for existance of a solution, linear independence of a set of vectors and the presence of "free" variables in a system among other things.

5. `MatrixMatrixMultiply` -- `MatrixMatrixMultiply(A,B)` multiplies the two matrices A and B --since matrix multiplication is not commutative, be careful of the order!

6. `MatrixInverse` -- For the inverse of a square matrix (if it exists), you can use either `MatrixInverse(A)` or `A^(-1)`. In fact, you may raise a matrix to any power using standard ^ notation -- this is useful when studying Markov chains and linear dynamical systems.

Eigenvalues and Eigenvectors

Computation of eigenvalues and eigenvectors is done with the `"Eigenvalues"` and `"Eigenvectors"` commands; first we'll compute and plot the characteristic polynomial to get some idea of the eigenvalues:

> $CharacteristicPolynomial(M, \lambda);$

$$66 + \lambda^3 - 12\lambda^2 + 23\lambda \qquad (19)$$

> $plot(\%, \lambda = -3 .. 10);$

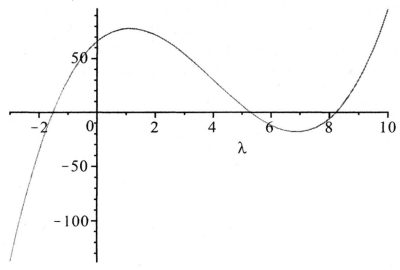

So the graph shows three real eigenvalues (the roots of the characteristic polynomial) for

115

our matrix, but note what Maple gives:

```
> Eigenvalues( M )
```

$$\left[\left[\frac{1}{3}\left(-405+15\,I\sqrt{1146}\right)^{1/3}+\frac{25}{\left(-405+15\,I\sqrt{1146}\right)^{1/3}}+4\right],\right. \tag{20}$$

$$\left[-\frac{1}{6}\left(-405+15\,I\sqrt{1146}\right)^{1/3}-\frac{25}{2\left(-405+15\,I\sqrt{1146}\right)^{1/3}}+4\right.$$

$$\left.+\frac{1}{2}I\sqrt{3}\left(\frac{1}{3}\left(-405+15\,I\sqrt{1146}\right)^{1/3}-\frac{25}{\left(-405+15\,I\sqrt{1146}\right)^{1/3}}\right)\right],$$

$$\left[-\frac{1}{6}\left(-405+15\,I\sqrt{1146}\right)^{1/3}-\frac{25}{2\left(-405+15\,I\sqrt{1146}\right)^{1/3}}+4\right.$$

$$\left.\left.-\frac{1}{2}I\sqrt{3}\left(\frac{1}{3}\left(-405+15\,I\sqrt{1146}\right)^{1/3}-\frac{25}{\left(-405+15\,I\sqrt{1146}\right)^{1/3}}\right)\right]\right]$$

A bit messy and note the presence of imaginary (I) values contrary to the appearance of the graph...we can use evalf to produce decimal values:

```
> evalf(%)
Warning, inserted missing semicolon at end of statement
```

$$\begin{bmatrix} 8.232195769 - 1.\,10^{-9}\,I \\ -1.517037347 - 6.660254040\,10^{-10}\,I \\ 5.284841577 + 1.066025404\,10^{-9}\,I \end{bmatrix} \tag{21}$$

so we have three real eigenvalues that Maple shows as complex: the key is that the imaginary parts are too small to be anything other than a result of computational errors due to roundoff. To get the eigenvectors (we'll use another matrix since the eigenvectors of M are complicated), use Eigenvectors whose output also gives the eigenvalues:

$$> MM := \begin{bmatrix} 1 & 2 & 1 \\ 6 & -1 & 0 \\ -1 & -2 & -1 \end{bmatrix}$$

$$MM := \begin{bmatrix} 1 & 2 & 1 \\ 6 & -1 & 0 \\ -1 & -2 & -1 \end{bmatrix} \tag{22}$$

```
> Eigenvectors ( MM )
```

116

$$\begin{bmatrix} 0 \\ -4 \\ 3 \end{bmatrix}, \begin{bmatrix} -\dfrac{1}{13} & -1 & -1 \\ -\dfrac{6}{13} & 2 & -\dfrac{3}{2} \\ 1 & 1 & 1 \end{bmatrix} \qquad (23)$$

> $evals := \%[1]; \; evects := \%\%[2]$

$$evals := \begin{bmatrix} 0 \\ -4 \\ 3 \end{bmatrix}$$

$$evects := \begin{bmatrix} -\dfrac{1}{13} & -1 & -1 \\ -\dfrac{6}{13} & 2 & -\dfrac{3}{2} \\ 1 & 1 & 1 \end{bmatrix} \qquad (24)$$

The double % is needed to pick out the matrix of eigenvectors since the assignment of the eigenvalue vector to evals produces an output, making the output of Eigenvectors the second output back. Note that the eigenvalues are the entries in the vector (0, -4, 3) and the corresponding eigenvectors sre the corresponding COLUMNS of the matrix (e.g., the eigenvector corresponding to $\lambda=0$ is $\begin{bmatrix} -\dfrac{1}{13} \\ -\dfrac{6}{13} \\ 1 \end{bmatrix}$ and so on. Also note that the matrix of eigenvectors is the matrix that diagonalizes the original matrix MM: evects^(-1)*MM* evects) = D:

> $MatrixInverse(evects).MM.evects$

$$\begin{bmatrix} 0 & 0 & 0 \\ 0 & -4 & 0 \\ 0 & 0 & 3 \end{bmatrix} \qquad (25)$$

giving a diagonal matrix containing the eigenvalues in the same order as the corresponding eigenvectors as expected.

General hints:

The matrix functions in Maple are generally pretty well-behaved. The thing that goes wrong most often is that people forget to use evalm sometimes -- when you get just the name of the matrix in response to typing its name as a command this is usually the reason.

Maple uses exact rational arithmetic in matrix computations unless you put some "floating point" numbers (i.e., numbers with decimal points) in the problem. Floating point computations are usually faster, so even if your problem involves only whole numbers, it is sometimes a good idea to express 3 as 3.0 etc.. if the computations are going too slowly. The down side is that extensive computations with floating point numbers are subject to a form of computational error due to rounding of intermediate calculations. This is the source of the (very) small imaginary parts of the answers to the eigenvalues command in (14) above

laplace (and invlaplace)

Maple has a pair of commands, `laplace` and `invlaplace` which are used to calculate Laplace transforms (and inverse Laplace transforms). The use of these commands is fairly straightforward -- Maple knows the formulas in the standard tables of Laplace transforms, as well as the operational properties (convolutions, derivatives, products, etc..), so these two commands can be applied to equations as well as to expressions.

The use of the commands is easiest to understand based on examples. But before we use them, because they are in Maple's integral transforms library (called `inttrans`), we must execute the command:

```
>  restart;
>  with(inttrans);
```
$$[\textit{addtable, fourier, fouriercos, fouriersin, hankel, hilbert, invfourier, invhilbert, invlaplace,}$$
$$\textit{invmellin, laplace, mellin, savetable}\,] \tag{1}$$

Then, to calculate the Laplace transform of the expression `t^3`, we enter:
```
>  laplace(t^3,t,s);
```
$$\frac{6}{s^4} \tag{2}$$

The syntax of the command requires three things between the parentheses: first, the expression whose Laplace transform is being taken, second, the name of the variable in the expression (in case other parameters are involved) -- usually this variable is t or x. Last is the name of the variable to be used in the expression of the Laplace transform (usually s or p) -- any variable may be used, as long as it doesn't conflict with a name already in use.

It is possible to take the Laplace transform of differential or integral equations -- when doing so it is important to note that, just as with `dsolve`, it is important to indicate which letters stand for functions by writing, for instance $y(t)$ rather than just y:

```
> laplace(diff(y(t),t)=3*y(t)+exp(-t),t,s);
```

$$s\,laplace(\,y(t),t,s) - y(0) = 3\,laplace(\,y(t),t,s) + \frac{1}{1+s} \tag{3}$$

Notice that in this case, Maple has applied several of the operational properties of Laplace transforms -- that of derivatives on the left side, and the one for exponentials and shift operators on the right.

One way to proceed with solving the differential equation is to solve the algebraic equation above for `laplace(y(t),t,s)` :

```
> solve(%,laplace(y(t),t,s));
```

$$\frac{y(0) + y(0)\,s + 1}{-2\,s + s^2 - 3} \tag{4}$$

and then to take the inverse Laplace transform with invlaplace:

```
> invlaplace(%,s,t);
```

$$-\frac{1}{4}\,e^{-t} + \frac{1}{4}\,e^{3t}\,(4\,y(0) + 1) \tag{5}$$

This gives the solution in terms of the initial condition, $y(0)$. On the other hand, the simplest way to get Maple to solve the differential equation in preceding example by Laplace transforms is to use the `dsolve` command with the "method=laplace" option, as follows:

```
> dsolve(diff(y(t),t)=3*y(t)+exp(-t),y(t),method=laplace);
```

$$y(t) = -\frac{1}{4}\,e^{-t} + \frac{1}{4}\,e^{3t}\,(4\,y(0) + 1) \tag{6}$$

As you undoubtedly already noticed, the `invlaplace` command undoes Laplace transforms -- we must tell this command about the variables, too but in the opposite order:

```
> invlaplace(2/(s^2+5),s,t);
```

$$\frac{2}{5}\,\sqrt{5}\,\sin(\sqrt{5}\,t) \tag{7}$$

Two functions that come up in the context of working with Laplace transforms are the Dirac delta and the unit step function (or Heaviside function). Maple understands these functions and their Laplace transforms. Their names in Maple are `Dirac(t)` and `Heaviside(t)` respectively:

```
> plot(Heaviside(t-3),t=0..5,discont=true,thickness=3);
```

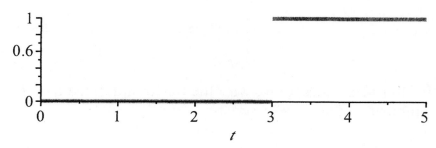

```
> laplace(Dirac(t-4),t,s);
```

$$e^{-4s} \qquad (8)$$

```
> laplace(Heaviside(t - 4), t, s);
```

$$\frac{e^{-4s}}{s} \qquad (9)$$

It is useful to note the following relationship between the Heaviside function and Dirac Delta:

```
> diff(Heaviside(t-2),t);
```

$$\mathrm{Dirac}(t-2) \qquad (10)$$

Consider the following piecewise function: $f(t) = 70$, $0 \leq t \leq 5$ and $50, t > 5$; it can be written as follows using the Heavisude function:

```
>  rs := (Heaviside(t) - Heaviside(t - 5))·70 + Heaviside(t - 5)·50;
```

$$rs := 70\,\mathrm{Heaviside}(t) - 20\,\mathrm{Heaviside}(t-5) \qquad (11)$$

```
> plot(rs, t=0..10, discont= true, thickness=2);
```

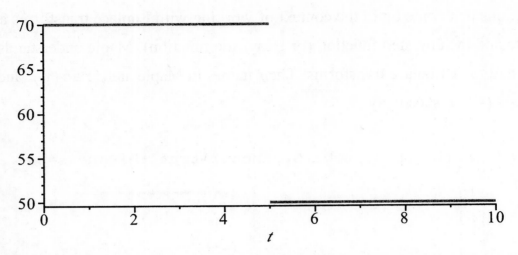

Now we solve Newton's Law of cooling with the function defined in (11) as the right hand side as the ambient temperature function:

```
>  eqn := diff ( y( t), t) + 0.05·y( t) = rs;
```

$$eqn := \frac{d}{dt} y(t) + 0.05\, y(t) = 70\, \text{Heaviside}(t) - 20\, \text{Heaviside}(t - 5) \qquad \textbf{(12)}$$

```
>  dsolve( { eqn, y( 0) = 98.6}, { y( t) }, method = laplace)
```

$$y(t) = -\frac{6507}{5}\, e^{-\frac{1}{20} t} + 1400 - 400\, \text{Heaviside}(t - 5) \left(1 - e^{-\frac{1}{20} t + \frac{1}{4}} \right) \qquad \textbf{(13)}$$

```
>  yy := rhs( %);
```

$$yy := -\frac{6507}{5}\, e^{-\frac{1}{20} t} + 1400 - 400\, \text{Heaviside}(t - 5) \left(1 - e^{-\frac{1}{20} t + \frac{1}{4}} \right) \qquad \textbf{(14)}$$

```
>  plot( yy, t = 0 ..10);
```

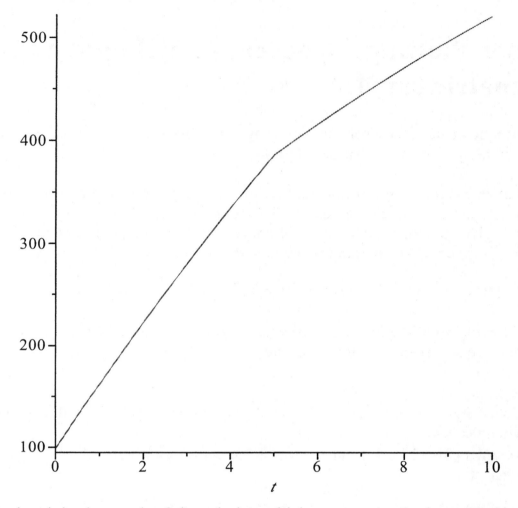

Note the break in the graph of the solution which occurs at $t = 5$ where the shange in the fuunction on the right side of the equation has a jump discontinuity. Laplace transform methods are particularly useful in such cases.

>

Fancier Plotting: spacecurve, fieldplot and parametric surface

This section describes two specialized plotting functions and an advanced use of **plot3d** all of which are part of Maple's **plots** library.

1. **spacecurve** - is the Maple command used for plotting curves in three-dimensional space. In 3D, curves can be obtained by intersecting surfaces, but it is much more common to give parametrized versions of curves. For example, consider the line in three dimensions is given by the parametric equations:

$$x=3+2*t \qquad y=4+t \qquad z=1-t.$$

To draw the line with Maple, using spacecurve, you proceed as follows--load the **plots** library then use spacecurve to draw the line:

```
>  with( plots) :
        #loads entire library so the commands used in this section are all available
        when needed
>  spacecurve([3 + 2 * t, 4 + t, 1 − t], t=−3 ..3, axes = normal, thickness = 3, color
        = black);
```

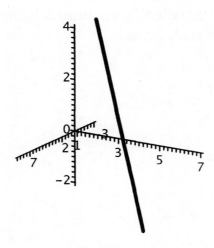

It is very common to want to combine a spacecurve plot with a plot of a surface. To combine 3D plots, one uses the display3d command just as with combination of surface

124

plots (again, see the section of this manual on plot3d for more detail). For example, here is a plot of a surface and one of the normal lines to it:

> $F := plot3d(x^2 + y^2, x=-2..2, y=-2..2)$:

The normal line to this surface at the point (1,1,2) is given by parametric equations:

> $normalLine := [1 - 2 \cdot t, 1 - 2 \cdot t, 2 + t]$;

$$normalLine := [1 - 2\,t, 1 - 2\,t, 2 + t] \qquad \qquad \textbf{(1)}$$

> $G := spacecurve(normalLine, t=-2..2)$:

And now both graphs can be displayed together using **display3d** (the axes and orientation were added by using the usual options in the plot menu or in the drop-down menus shown once the plot is selected.

> $display3d(\{F, G\})$;

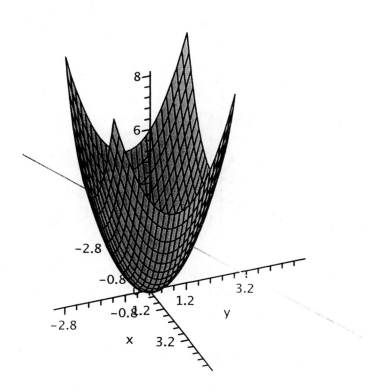

2. **fieldplot** - is used to draw pictures of vector fields in two dimensions and **fieldplot3d** draws 3D vector fields.

For example, let's consider the vector field x*i+y*j --- in Maple we write this as:

$>$ *vField* $:= [x, y]$

$$vField := [x, y] \qquad (2)$$

To draw the vector field, we use **fieldplot**:

$>$ *fieldplot*(*vField*, $x=-1..1, y=-1..1$);

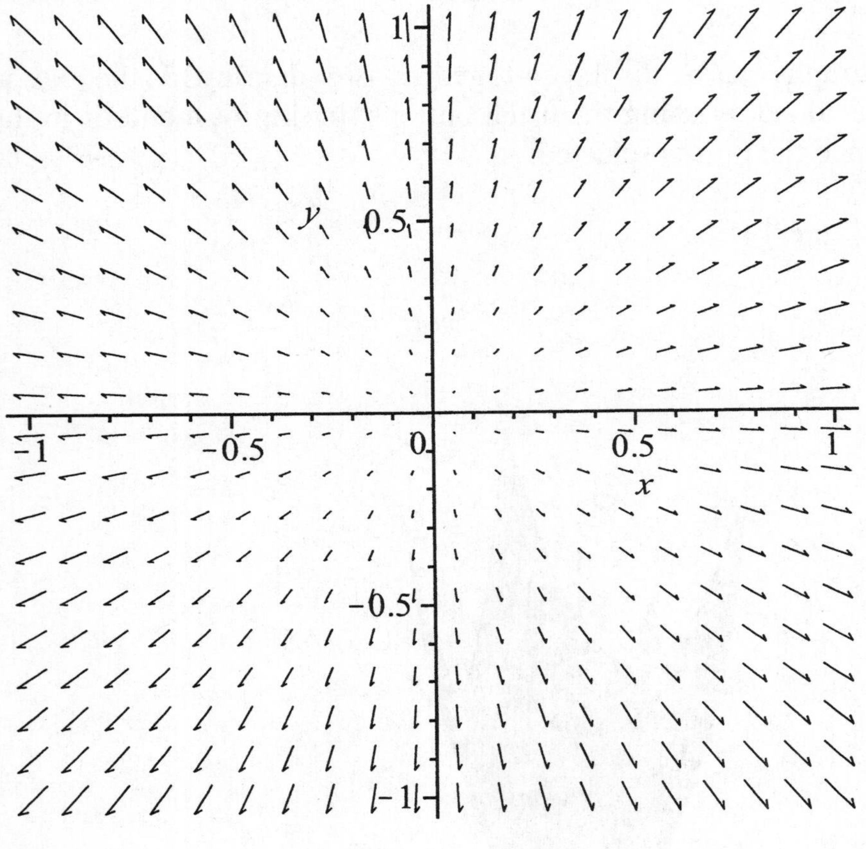

Plots of vector fields can be combined with plots of curves in the plane using a similar technique to that above for the surface and its normal using the **plot** and **fieldplot** commands, but is not illustrated here.

Three-D vector fields can be plotted using **fieldplot3d**, for example:

$>$ *vectorField* $:= [x, y, -2 \cdot z]$;

$$vectorField := [x, y, -2z] \qquad (3)$$

$>$ *fieldplot3d*(*vectorField*, $x=-1..1, y=-1..1, z=-1..1$);

126

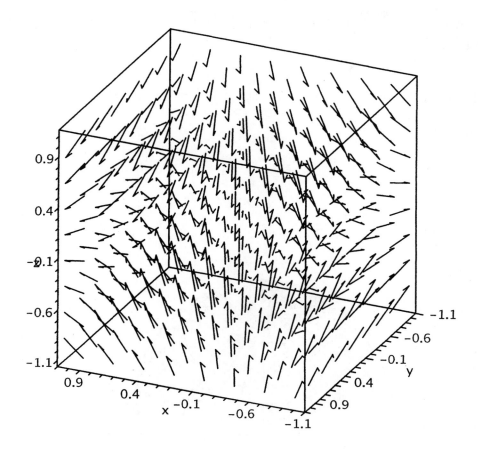

Axes were added and the orientation set in the usual way--select the plot by clicking in it and choosing the appropriate options from the **plot** menu.

Pictures of 3d vectorfields can be difficult to understand -- it is sometime instructive to watch as they are drawn by Maple. Again, it is possible to use the 3d plotting options to change perspectives, add axes, etc.. Also, one can combine a fieldplot3d with the plot of a curve or surface using display3d.

3. **Parametric surfaces**. It is often necessary when computing surface integrals to parametrize the surface using variables other than x, y or z. Maple (as part of the plot3d command) can draw parametrized surfaces, and this is useful sometimes for visualization and to make sure you've got the parametrization right. There are some examples of this in the "solved problems" section of this manual. Here is another -- note that the pieces of the parametrization go into obvious places, very analogous to parametric plotting of curves in 2 and 3 dimensions (discussed above and elsewhere in this manual). Here is the sphere of radius 2 centered at the point (0,0,1), which is given parametrically (see the

section of the text on spherical coordinates) by:

x=2*cos(u)*cos(v), y=2*cos(u)*sin(v), z=1+2*sin(u) as u goes from -Pi/2 to Pi/2 and v
goes from 0 to 2*Pi:

$$> \quad plot3d\left(\; [\,2\cdot\cos(u)\cdot\cos(v),\, 2\cdot\cos(u)\cdot\sin(v),\, 1+2\cdot\sin(u)\,],\, u = -\frac{\mathrm{Pi}}{2}\,..\frac{\mathrm{Pi}}{2},\, v \right.$$

$$\left. =0\,..2\cdot\mathrm{Pi}\right);$$

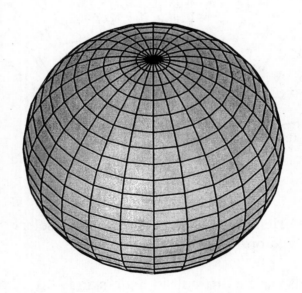

One thing to notice about the syntax is that (as opposed to parametric plotting of curves),
the range expressions u = - Pi/2..Pi/2 and v = 0..2*Pi go outside of the square brackets
rather than inside.

4. **Plotting surfaces over general regions.** Variable limits can be specified for one of
the independent variables in a 3D surface plot to show only that portion of a surface over
a well defined region in the x-y plane. The next plot shows only that part of the
paraboloid $z=x^2+y^2$ over the region defined by $-3 \le x \le 3$, $0 \le y \le 1+x$. This will be

128

graphed twice--once oriented to show the region, then once to show the surface over the region

> $plot3d\left(x^2 + y^2, x = -3 .. 3, y = 0 .. 1 + x\right);$

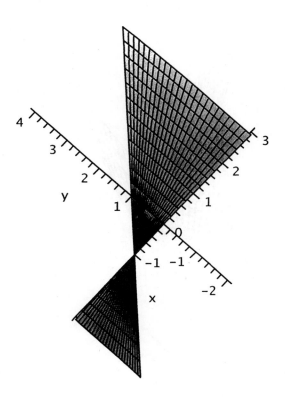

> $plot3d\left(x^2 + y^2, x = -3 .. 3, y = 0 .. 1 + x, axes = normal\right);$

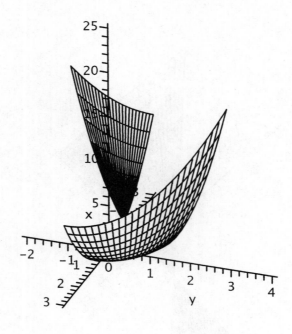

Complex numbers in Maple
(I, evalc, etc..)

You will undoubtedly have encountered some complex numbers in Maple long before you begin studying them seriously in Math 241. For example, solving polynomial equations often leads to complex numbers:

```
> restart;
> solve(x^2+3*x+11=0,x);
```

$$-\frac{3}{2} + \frac{1}{2} I \sqrt{35}, \; -\frac{3}{2} - \frac{1}{2} I \sqrt{35} \qquad (1)$$

Maple uses a capital I to represent the square root of -1 (commonly called i in mathematics texts and sometimes called j in engineering texts). You use I to input complex numbers as well:

```
> z:=4+5*I; w:=3-2*I;
```

$$z := 4 + 5 I \qquad (2)$$
$$w := 3 - 2 I$$

All of the basic arithmetic and standard functions work on complex numbers -- so we can add, subtract, multiply, divide, take exponentials, sines, Bessel functions, etc.. of complex numbers:

```
> z+w; z^2; z/w; exp(z);
```

$$7 + 3 I \qquad (3)$$
$$-9 + 40 I$$
$$\frac{2}{13} + \frac{23}{13} I$$
$$e^{(4 + 5 I)}$$

To force Maple to report a complex number in "a+bI" format, there is the command `evalc` (for "evaluate as a complex number" -- it is similar to `evalf` which forces decimal, or floating point, evaluation):

```
> evalc(exp(z));
```

$$e^4 \cos(5) + I e^4 \sin(5) \tag{4}$$

A few other complex functions Maple knows about are: `conjugate`, `argument`, and `abs`. They do the obvious things:

```
> conjugate(z); argument(w); abs(z);
```

$$\bar{z} \tag{5}$$

$$-\arctan\left(\frac{2}{3}\right)$$

$$|z|$$

The absolute value in this case is the complex absolute value (or modulus -- the distance from the complex number to the origin in the Argand plane).

Maple understands complex limits -- to calculate them, use the "complex" option in the `limit` command (we cleared the value of z before executing the following):

```
> z:='z':
> limit((exp(I*z)-1)/z,z=0,complex);
```

$$I \tag{6}$$

Complex derivatives work the same in Maple as ordinary real derivatives -- integrals are contour integrals, of course , which require parametrization of the contour and substitution of the parametrization into dz. For examples of this see the demonstration m241demo9 and the section of this manual containing answers to selected Math 241 problems.

Finally, for exploring the geometry of complex functions as mappings from the plane to itself (or of the z-plane to the w-plane), there is the `conformal` command in the "`plots`" library. (By "mapping, we mean a transformation that takes each point on the plane to another point on the plane. If there are lines on the plane to begin with, these lines will be transformed into other lines or curves.) We load the `conformal` command by typing:

```
>  with(plots,conformal);
```

$$[\,conformal\,]$$

(7)

The conformal command illustrates what happens to lines parallel to the coordinate axes when a complex function is applied. In the following example, the mapping from z to exp(z) takes the vertical lines on the Cartesian plane to the (red) circles in the picture. The mapping also takes the horizontal lines to the (green) radial lines in the picture.

```
>  conformal(exp(z),z=-3-Pi*I..1+Pi*I);
```

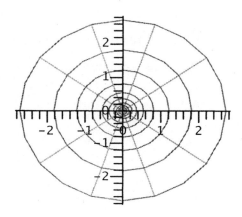

Note that this is the transformation from rectangular to polar coordinates. The syntax of the `conformal` command is: first, you supply the complex expression that is to be applied, and then give the domain -- the domain is always a rectangle in the complex plane, and you need to supply the (complex) names of the points at the lower left corner (`-3-Pi*I` in this case) and the upper right corner (`1+Pi*I` in this case) of the rectangle.

To see how complex mappings transform the polar coordinate grid, you can compose the mapping in question with the exponential function. As an example, suppose we want to know what the mapping `sqrt(1+z^2)` does to the unit disk. Then we could consider:

133

```
> conformal(sqrt(1+(exp(z)^2)),z=-3-Pi*I..1+Pi*I);
```

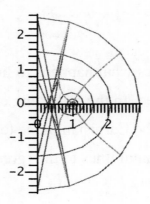

```
>
```

You can see that the result is contained in the right half plane, and some indication is given of how it gets there, but more thought would be needed for a complete explanation.

The VectorCalculus Package

The VectorCalculus package is designed to simplify problems involving computation with vectors, vector fields, multiple variable functions and parametric curves. It is capable of doing vector arithmetic in 37 different coordinate systems including the usual Cartesian systems in 2, 3 , 4 and more dimensions, polar coordinates, cylindrical coordinates and spherical coordinates. For more information on the coordinate systems programmed into Maple, try the Help command ?Coordinates. You also have the ability to define your own coordinate system. This package is fully compatible with the LinearAlgebra package described elsewhere in this manual.

Additional capabilities include the ability to perform "del" operations (div, grad and curl), compute multiple integrals over regions in the *x-y* plane, or over regions in 3-space, compute line and surface integrals and various differential-geometric properties of curves plus many other capabilities, some of which are illustrated below.

Begin, as usual, by loading the VectorCalculus package (and be careful to capitalize and spell the commands as Maple expects or the results may be unpredictable or, more likely, there will be no results at all.

with(*VectorCalculus*);

$[\&x, *, +, -, ., <, >, <|>, AddCoordinates, ArcLength, BasisFormat, Binormal, CrossProd,$ (1)
    CrossProduct, Curl, Curvature, D, Del, DirectionalDiff, Divergence, DotProd, DotProduct, Flux
    , GetCoordinateParameters, GetCoordinates, Gradient, Hessian, Jacobian, Laplacian, LineInt,
    MapToBasis, Nabla, Norm, Normalize, PathInt, PrincipalNormal, RadiusOfCurvature,
    ScalarPotential, SetCoordinateParameters, SetCoordinates, SurfaceInt, TNBFrame, Tangent,
    TangentLine, TangentPlane, TangentVector, Torsion, Vector, VectorField, VectorPotential,
    Wronskian, diff, evalVF, int, limit, series]

Lets start with setting coordinates, the command for which is SetCoordinates. This command takes two parameters: 1) an (optional) vector whose coordinates are to be set , and 2) the name of the coordinate system to use plus an optional list of coordinate name. If only the name of the coordinate system is specified, thaen that system becomes the default system for subsequent calculations until it is changed by another call to SetCoordinates. The coordinate systems we will use are: 2D-cartesian, polar; 3D-cartesian, cylindrical and spherical.
To set the default system to 3D cartesian coordinates:

SetCoordinates(*cartesian*[*x, y, z*]);

$$cartesian_{x,\ y,\ z} \qquad\qquad (2)$$

This example includes the optional list of coordinate identifiers. Next, define a vector in 3 space(vectors defined in the way shown can be used in the routines contained in the LinearAlgebra package. For Example:

v := *Vector*([1, 2, 3]);   (3)

$$e_x + 2e_y + 3e_z \tag{3}$$

Note that the vector is written out in terms of the standard basis vectors of the cartesian system; e[x] for instance is [1, 0, 0], e[y] = [0, 1, 0] and e[z] = [0,0,1].

The MapToBasis command converts a vector in one system to an equivalent vector in another. An example (note that the parameters are the vector to be converted and then the coordinate system):
MapToBasis(*v, spherical*[*r*, ϕ, θ]);

$$\left(\sqrt{14}\right)e_r + \left(\arctan\left(\frac{1}{3}\sqrt{5}\right)\right)e_\phi + (\arctan(2))e_\theta \tag{4}$$

gives the spherical coordinate form of the cartesian vector *v*.

The VectorField command generates vector fields in a usable form, for example:

$$VF := VectorField(<\sin(x), \cos(y), \sin(z)>);$$
$$(\sin(x))e_x + (\cos(y))e_y + (\sin(z))e_z \tag{5}$$

Note that the field is given in the current default coordinate system, cartesian. The evalVF command will evaluate a vector field for some particular vector(Note that the parameters are the vector field followed by the vector):
evalVF(*VF*, < π, π, π >);

$$0e_x - e_y + 0e_z \tag{6}$$

The fieldplot and fieldplot3d commands of the plots package can be used to display vector fields.

with(*plots*);
[*Interactive, animate, animate3d, animatecurve, arrow, changecoords, complexplot, complexplot3d,* (7)
    conformal, conformal3d, contourplot, contourplot3d, coordplot, coordplot3d, cylinderplot,
    densityplot, display, display3d, fieldplot, fieldplot3d, gradplot, gradplot3d, graphplot3d,
    implicitplot, implicitplot3d, inequal, interactive, interactiveparams, listcontplot, listcontplot3d,
    listdensityplot, listplot, listplot3d, loglogplot, logplot, matrixplot, multiple, odeplot, pareto,
    plotcompare, pointplot, pointplot3d, polarplot, polygonplot, polygonplot3d, polyhedra_supported
    , polyhedraplot, replot, rootlocus, semilogplot, setoptions, setoptions3d, spacecurve,
    sparsematrixplot, sphereplot, surfdata, textplot, textplot3d, tubeplot]
fieldplot3d(*VF, x* = $-Pi..\pi, y = -Pi..\pi, z = -Pi..\pi, scaling = constrained, axes = boxed$);

136

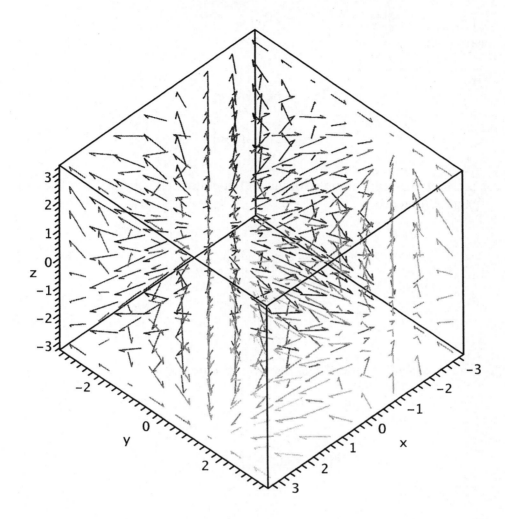

Computing dot and cross products is simple as the following examples illustrate. The Maple VectorCalculus commands are DotProduct (alias: DotProd) or '.' and CrossProduct or '&x'. When combined with the Del command, these operators can produce the curl or divergence of a vector field:

First define a couple of vectors for use in these examples:

$v := Vector(<2, 3, 4>);$

$$2e_x + 3e_y + 4e_z \qquad\qquad (8)$$

$w := Vector(<5, -6, 7>);$

$$5e_x - 6e_y + 7e_z \qquad\qquad (9)$$

Next compute the dot product of v & w:

$DotProduct(v, w);$

$$20 \qquad\qquad (10)$$

alternately:

v.w;

20

(11)

And now the crossproduct:

CrossProduct(*v*, *w*);

$$45e_x + 6e_y - 27e_z$$

(12)

w & *x v*;

$$-45e_x - 6e_y + 27e_z$$

(13)

The dot and cross product operators along with the Del operator can be applied to vector fields to compute their curl and divergence:

Curl(*VF*);

$$0e_x + 0e_y + 0e_z$$

(14)

or

Del & *x VF*;

$$0e_x + 0e_y + 0e_z$$

(15)

which shows VF is a conservative vector field because its curl is 0.

Also:

Divergence(*VF*);

$$\cos(x) - \sin(y) + \cos(z)$$

(16)

or

Del.VF;

$$\cos(x) - \sin(y) + \cos(z)$$

(17)

produce the divergence of the vector field VF.

Multivariable Calculus:

Multivariable differential calculus is easily performed with the VectorCalculus package. Gradients of functions are computed via the Gradient command as shown in this example:

$f := x^3 - 2 \cdot y^2 + sin(z)$;

$$x^3 - 2y^2 + \sin(z)$$

(18)

Gradient(*f*);

$$3x^2 e_x - 4ye_y + (\cos(z))e_z$$

(19)

Directional derivatives are easily computed via the DirrectionalDiff command:

$DirectionalDiff(f, < 1, 2, 1 >);$

$$\frac{1}{6} \sqrt{6} \left(3 x^2 - 8 y + \cos(z) \right) \tag{20}$$

Note that the direction vector supplied must have the correct number of components and need not be normalized (i.e., reduced to a unit vector) that is done automatically by DirectionalDiff.

Now a classic problem--constrained optimization. Suppose you want to maximize the product xyz subject to the constraint that $2x + 2y + z$ not exceed 100. This is a classic problem easily solved by the method of Lagrange multipliers. We proceed as follows:

Let the function to be maximized be

$V := x \cdot y \cdot z;$

$$x\,y\,z \tag{21}$$

and the constraint is then $2x + 2y + z = 100$:

$g := 2 \cdot x + 2 \cdot y + z - 100;$

$$-100 + 2\,x + 2\,y + z \tag{22}$$

so the Lagrangian for the problem becomes:

$Lagr := V - \lambda \cdot g;$

$$x\,y\,z - \lambda\,(-100 + 2\,x + 2\,y + z) \tag{23}$$

Next compute the gradient of the Lagrangian:

$GradLagr := Gradient(Lagr);$

$$(y\,z - 2\,\lambda)e_x + (x\,z - 2\,\lambda)e_y + (x\,y - \lambda)e_z \tag{24}$$

and solve g=0, GradLagr=0:

$solve(\{g = 0, seq(GradLagr[j] = 0, j = 1..3)\}, \{x, y, z, \lambda\});$

$$\{y = 0, x = 0, z = 100, \lambda = 0\}, \{z = 0, x = 50, y = 0, \lambda = 0\}, \{z = 0, x = 0, y = 50, \lambda = 0\}, \tag{25}$$
$$\left\{ x = \frac{50}{3}, y = \frac{50}{3}, z = \frac{100}{3}, \lambda = \frac{2500}{9} \right\}$$

There are four possible solutions, a quick inspection of which shows that three are minimasince one or more of x, y or z are zero, so the last solution in the set must be the maximum sought.

Integrating real and vector functions over regions in two and three space is relatively simple with the VectorCalculus package so long as the region can be described in terms Maple can understand. Suppose, for inatance, you wanted to compute the integral of x^2*y^3 over the circle centered at the origin of radius 2. The VectorCalculus package adds to the int command the ability to recognize such integrals...in this instance:

139

$$int\left(x^2 \cdot y^3, \ [x, y] = Circle(<0, 0>, 2)\right);$$

$$0$$

(26)

or the same function over a rectangle with vertices (0, 2), (0, -3), (0, -3), and (0, 2):

$$int\left(x^2 \cdot y^3, \ [x, y] = Rectangle(0..2, \ -3..2)\right);$$

$$\frac{-130}{3}$$

(27)

A similar problem in 3 space: integrate x^2y^3z^(-1) over the unit sphere centered at (1, 2, 3):

$$int\left(x^2 y^3 z^{(-1)}, \ [x, y, z] = Sphere(<1, \ 2, \ 3>, \ 1)\right);$$

$$32\,\pi\ln(2) - \frac{86}{5}\,\pi$$

(28)

Line and Surface Integrals

The vector calculus package has built in procedures to compute line integrals and surface integrals.

Line integrals are evaluated by the command LineInt(F, dom, inert). For the LineInt command we have the following:
   The parameters are:

   F   - 'Vector'(algebraic) or procedure; specifies the VectorField to integrate

   dom - unevaluated function call; specifies the path of integration

   inert - (optional) name; specify that the integral representation is to be returned

The path of integration is specified by giving either an arc of an ellipse or a circle{form: Arc(object,start angle, end angle) here object is either a circle or an ellipse structure (equation of the graph)}, a Circle {form: Circle(center, radius) or Circle3D(center, radius,normal) where normal is a vector normal to the plane containing the circle}, an Ellipse {formEllipse(eqn) where eqn is the equation of an ellipse such that the ellipse is given by eqn=0.}, a line {form: Line(p1,p2) where p1 and p2 are the initial and final points of the line segment},a set of (connected) line segments {form: LineSegments(p1, p2, p3, ..., pk) where pi are the points where the line segments begin and end, If the segments form a polygon, pk = p1) or a general path {form: Path(v, rng, [c]) where v is a vector representing the parameterized path, rng is the range ov values for the parameter used to define the path and the optional parameter [c] if specified is the coordinate system in which the path is to be interpreted}.

The LineInt(F, dom, inert) command returns the integral form of the line integral of the F over dom.

For Example:

$$SetCoordinates(cartesian[x, y]);$$

$$cartesian_{x, y}$$

(29)

$$FF := VectorField(<-y, x>);$$

(30)

$$-y e_x + (x) e_y \tag{30}$$

Now integrate the vector field over the triangular path joining (0,0), (2,0)and (0,3):

LineInt(FF, LineSegments(< 0, 0 >, < 2, 0 >, < 0, 3 >, < 0, 0 >));
$$6 \tag{31}$$

Now try an arc of a circle:

LineInt(FF, Arc(Ellipse($x^2 + y^2 - 16$), 0, 2));
$$\frac{8\left(2\tan(2) + \pi + \pi\tan(2)^2\right)}{1 + \tan(2)^2} \tag{32}$$

evalf(%);
$$19.07832126 \tag{33}$$

Surface integrals can be computed similarly. From the Maple Help system of the SurfaceInt command we have the following description of the paramenters:

   The SurfaceInt(f, dom) command computes the surface integral of the function f over the surface specified on the right side of dom. The left side of dom is the list of variables of the function f.

   Surfaces are represented by unevaluated function calls. The possible surfaces are Box(r1, r2, r3), Sphere(cen, rad), and Surface(v).

        Box(r1, r2, r3)

             Each ri must have type algebraic..algebraic. These represent the sides of the box, and the surface integral taken over each face of the box.

        Sphere(cen, rad)

             The first parameter of Sphere, cen, must have type 'Vector'(3, algebraic) and rad must have type algebraic. These represent the center and radius of the sphere, respectively. If a coordinate   system attribute is specified on cen, the center is interpreted in this coordinate system.

        Surface(v)

             The first argument of v must have type 'Vector'(3, algebraic). The second argument can be of the form list(name) = region where the names of the two parameters are in the list and the   region of the second argument is any valid two dimensional region that VectorCalculus:-int accepts, or an equation of the form name=range. If the region is in the form name= range, the   third argument, range is also of the form name= range. This gives explicit ranges to the two parameters.

   Finally, an optional fourth argument can be coords=name or coordinates=name. It is the coordinate system in which v is interpreted.

   The SurfaceInt(f, dom, inert) command returns the integral form of the surface integral of f over dom.

$SetCoordinates\big(cartesian_{x,y,z}\big);$

$$cartesian_{x,y,z} \tag{34}$$

$SurfaceInt(x \cdot y \cdot z, \ [x, y, z] = Sphere(\ <1, 1, 1>, 5));$

$$100\,\pi \tag{35}$$

$SurfaceInt(sin(x \cdot y \cdot z), \ [x, y, z] = Box(1\,..2, \ 1\,..2, \ 0\,..3));$

$$3\ln(2) + \frac{5}{3}\,Ci(3) - \frac{1}{3}\,Ci(6) - \frac{4}{3}\,Ci(12) \tag{36}$$

$evalf(\%);$

$$2.367883609 \tag{37}$$

Here Ci is the cosine integral defined by Ci(x) = gamma + ln(x) + int((cos(t)-1)/t, t=0..x).

142

Sample Final Examinations From Recent Years

In this section are several final examinations given at the end of Math 240 and 241. The questions on these exams form a part of the core problem set. Since most final exams tend to be similar to these, you can use them as practice exams for your final. As part of the core problem set, your instructor may choose to assign some of these problems as homework.

Solutions for selected exams and additional exams may be found on the course websites for Math 240 and for Math 241, but are not included here.

NAME: _____   **PENN ID#:** _____

(201) (202) (203) (204)	Math 240-001	Matthew WIENER/Peter DALAKOV
(211) (212) (213) (214)	Math 240-002	Stéphane SABOURAU/Andrei PAVELESCU
(221) (222) (223) (224)	Math 240-003	Jayant LAL/Shea VICK

Instructions.

Please write your name and Penn ID in the space provided above, and fill in the oval identifying your section and instructors. You will have two hours to complete this exam.

You are allowed to use one $8\frac{1}{2} \times 11$ sheet, both sides, for notes you wrote yourself. You are not allowed to use calculators.

Do not detach this sheet from the body of the exam.

This is a multiple-choice test, but you must show your work. Blind guessing will not be credited.

Please mark your answer on both the front cover and on the problem itself. If you change an answer, be absolutely clear which choice is your final answer.

All of the problems have exactly one correct answer.

All problems have equal weight. No partial credit will be given. No penalties for incorrect answers will be taken.

Questions 1-11					Questions 12-22				
1. (A) (B) (C) (D) (E)					12. (A) (B) (C) (D) (E)				
2. (A) (B) (C) (D) (E)					13. (A) (B) (C) (D) (E)				
3. (A) (B) (C) (D) (E)					14. (A) (B) (C) (D) (E)				
4. (A) (B) (C) (D) (E)					15. (A) (B) (C) (D) (E)				
5. (A) (B) (C) (D) (E)					16. (A) (B) (C) (D) (E)				
6. (A) (B) (C) (D) (E)					17. (A) (B) (C) (D) (E)				
7. (A) (B) (C) (D) (E)					18. (A) (B) (C) (D) (E)				
8. (A) (B) (C) (D) (E)					19. (A) (B) (C) (D) (E)				
9. (A) (B) (C) (D) (E)					20. (A) (B) (C) (D) (E)				
10. (A) (B) (C) (D) (E)					21. (A) (B) (C) (D) (E)				
11. (A) (B) (C) (D) (E)					22. (A) (B) (C) (D) (E)				

1. For the matrices A^{-1} and B^{-1} below, find $(AB)^{-1}$.

$$A^{-1} = \begin{pmatrix} 1 & 2 \\ 3 & 2 \end{pmatrix} \quad B^{-1} = \begin{pmatrix} 2 & 1 \\ 3 & 1 \end{pmatrix}$$

(A) $\begin{pmatrix} 8 & 12 \\ 12 & 5 \end{pmatrix}$ (B) $\begin{pmatrix} 8 & 3 \\ 12 & 5 \end{pmatrix}$ (C) $\begin{pmatrix} 5 & 6 \\ 6 & 8 \end{pmatrix}$ (D) $\begin{pmatrix} 5 & 8 \\ 8 & 6 \end{pmatrix}$

(E) This can't be done: one of A, B is singular, and AB is undefined.

2. Find $y(\pi)$, where y satisfies the differential equation

$$\frac{d^4y}{dx^4} - 16y = 0\,,$$

subject to the initial condition

$$y(0) = 1, \quad y'(0) = 0, \quad y''(0) = -4, \quad y'''(0) = 0\,.$$

As a reminder, $A^4 - 16 = (A^2 - 4)(A^2 + 4) = (A - 2)(A + 2)(A^2 + 4)$.

(A) 0   (B) 1   (C) $\frac{1}{2}e^{2\pi} + \frac{3}{2}$ (D) $\frac{1}{2}e^{2\pi} + \frac{1}{2}e^{-2\pi} - \frac{1}{2}$ (E) $\frac{1}{2}e^{2\pi} - \frac{1}{2}e^{-2\pi} + \frac{3}{2}$

3. Give the general solution to the differential equation

$$x^2 y'' - 2xy' + 2y = 0.$$

(A) $y = c_1 x^2 + c_2 x^3$ (B) $y = c_1 + c_2 x^{-2}$ (C) $y = c_1 x + c_2 x^3$

(D) $y = c_1 + c_2 x^2$ (E) $y = c_1 x + c_2 x^2$

4. Which of the following diagrams is the direction field for the differential equation $y' = xy$?

In the figures, the x-axis and the y-axis both run from -2 to 2.

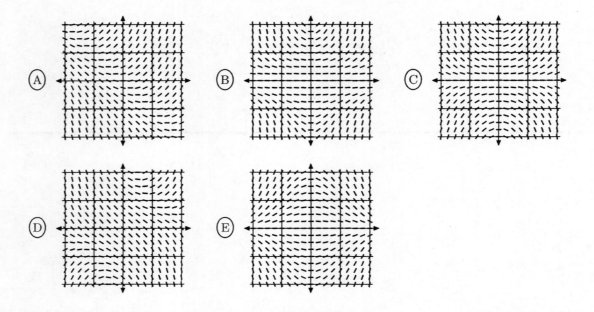

5. Evaluate the inverse Laplace transform

$$\mathcal{L}^{-1}\left\{\frac{4s+23}{s^2+4s+29}\right\}.$$

(A) $2e^{4t}\sin 5t + 3e^{4t}\cos 5t$ (B) $3e^{2t}\sin 5t - 2e^{2t}\cos 5t$ (C) $2e^{-2t}\sin 5t + 3e^{-2t}\cos 5t$

(D) $3e^{-2t}\sin 5t + 4e^{-2t}\cos 5t$ (E) $2e^{2t}\sin 5t + 2e^{2t}\cos 5t$

6. The differential equation

$$y' - 2y = e^{2t},$$

with initial condition $y(0) = 3$, has its solution expressible using inverse Laplace transforms as:

(A) $\mathcal{L}^{-1}\left\{\dfrac{3}{s-2}\right\} + \mathcal{L}^{-1}\left\{\dfrac{1}{(s-2)^2}\right\}$ (B) $\mathcal{L}^{-1}\left\{\dfrac{3}{s-2}\right\} + \mathcal{L}^{-1}\left\{\dfrac{1}{(s-1)}\right\}$

(C) $\mathcal{L}^{-1}\left\{\dfrac{2}{s-2}\right\} + \mathcal{L}^{-1}\left\{\dfrac{2}{(s-1)^2}\right\}$ (D) $\mathcal{L}^{-1}\left\{\dfrac{2}{s-2}\right\} - \mathcal{L}^{-1}\left\{\dfrac{1}{(s-2)^2}\right\}$

(E) $\mathcal{L}^{-1}\left\{\dfrac{1}{s-2}\right\} - \mathcal{L}^{-1}\left\{\dfrac{3}{(s-2)^2}\right\}$

7. If you solve the following system of differential equations

$$\begin{cases} x' = x + 3y \\ y' = 5x + 3y \end{cases}$$

subject to the initial condition $x(0) = 5$ and $y(0) = 3$, then $x(t)$ is given by:

(A) $x = e^{2t} + 4e^{5t}$ (B) $x = 3e^{-2t} + 2e^{6t}$ (C) $x = 2e^{-2t} + 3e^{6t}$

(D) $x = 3e^{2t} + 2e^{5t}$ (E) $x = 6e^{2t} - e^{3t}$

8. Find c_4, where $y = \sum_{k=0}^{\infty} c_k x^k$ is a solution to the differential equation

$$y'' - (1+x^2)y = 0\,,$$

subject to the initial condition $y(0) = 8$ and $y'(0) = -3$.

(A) 1   (B) 2   (C) 3   (D) 4   (E) 5

9. Find a recurrence relation for c_n, where $y = \sum_{k=0}^{\infty} c_k x^k$ is a solution to the differential equation

$$y'' + xy' + y = 0.$$

That is, give a formula for c_{n+2} in terms of c_n and/or c_{n+1}.

(A) $c_{n+2} = -\dfrac{c_n + c_{n+1}}{n}$

(B) $c_{n+2} = \dfrac{(2n-1)}{(n+1)(n+2)} c_n$

(C) $c_{n+2} = -\dfrac{c_n}{n+2}$

(D) $c_{n+2} = -\dfrac{c_n + c_{n+1}}{n(n+1)}$

(E) $c_{n+2} = -\dfrac{c_n}{2n(n-1)}$

10. Let $\mathcal{S}$ be the surface consisting of the boundary of the unit cube $0 \le x \le 1$, $0 \le y \le 1$, $0 \le z \le 1$, and let $\mathbf{F} = (e^x + z)\mathbf{i} + (y^2 - x)\mathbf{j} - xe^y\mathbf{k}$. Evaluate the outward flux (or divergence)

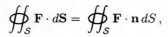

$$\oiint_{\mathcal{S}} \mathbf{F} \cdot d\mathbf{S} = \oiint_{\mathcal{S}} \mathbf{F} \cdot \mathbf{n}\, dS\,,$$

also written

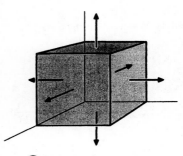

$$\oiint_{\mathcal{S}} (e^x + z)\, dy\, dz + (y^2 - x)\, dz\, dx - xe^y\, dx\, dy\,.$$

(A) $e - 2$ (B) e (C) $e + 2$ (D) $e + 3$ (E) $4 - e$

11. Find

$$\int_{C} (2x + e^y)\, dx + (3y^2 + xe^y)\, dy\,,$$

where C is the arc of the ellipse $x^2 + 4(y-2)^2 = 4$ from $(0,1)$ to $(2,2)$ in the counterclockwise direction.

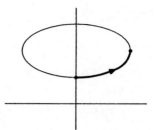

(A) $e^3 + 12$ (B) $3e - 7$ (C) $2e^2 + 11$ (D) $3e^2 + 14$ (E) $e^2 + 8$

12. Evaluate

$$\oint_C (e^x + 3y)\, dx + (4x + y^6)\, dy$$

where C is the circle $(x-2)^2 + (y-4)^2 = 1$, traversed counterclockwise.

(A) 0   (B) 1   (C) e (D) π (E) 4

13. A certain forced undamped oscillator is modelled by the differential equation

$$m\frac{d^2x}{dt^2} + 18x = 4\cos 3t \,.$$

What mass $m > 0$ corresponds to resonance, that is, $x(t)$ is unbounded as $t \to \infty$?

(A) $m = 1$ (B) $m = 2$ (C) $m = 3$ (D) $m = 4$ (E) $m = 5$

14. Compute the determinant

$$\begin{vmatrix} 0 & -1 & -3 \\ 2 & 3 & 3 \\ -2 & 1 & 1 \end{vmatrix}.$$

(A) -16 (B) -8 (C) 0 (D) 8 (E) 16

15. Solve for x in the system

$$x \ - \ y - 3z = 0$$
$$x + 3y + 3z = 2$$
$$y \ + \ z = -2$$

As a hint:

$$\begin{vmatrix} 1 & -1 & -3 \\ 1 & 3 & 3 \\ 0 & 1 & 1 \end{vmatrix} = -2$$

You can also use the previous problem.

(A) -8 (B) -4 (C) no solution   (D) 4   (E) 8

16. Compute the sum of the elements in the last column of A^{-1} where

$$A = \begin{pmatrix} 1 & 0 & 1 \\ -1 & 1 & 0 \\ 0 & -1 & 1 \end{pmatrix}.$$

(A) -1 (B) $-\dfrac{1}{2}$ (C) $\dfrac{1}{2}$ (D) 1 (E) A is actually singular, and A^{-1} is undefined.

17. If

$$\begin{vmatrix} a_1 & a_2 & a_3 \\ b_1 & b_2 & b_3 \\ c_1 & c_2 & c_3 \end{vmatrix} = x\,,$$

then

$$\begin{vmatrix} 2c_2 + a_2 & b_2 & -a_2 \\ 2c_1 + a_1 & b_1 & -a_1 \\ 2c_3 + a_3 & b_3 & -a_3 \end{vmatrix} = \;?$$

(A) 0   (B) $-x$ (C) $2x$ (D) $-2x$ (E) $3x$

18. Select a matrix with eigenvalues 0 and 2, and corresponding eigenvectors $\begin{pmatrix} 1 \\ 2 \end{pmatrix}$, $\begin{pmatrix} 1 \\ 3 \end{pmatrix}$.

Ⓐ $\begin{pmatrix} -4 & 2 \\ -12 & 6 \end{pmatrix}$ Ⓑ $\begin{pmatrix} -2 & 1 \\ -8 & 4 \end{pmatrix}$ Ⓒ $\begin{pmatrix} -4 & -12 \\ 2 & 6 \end{pmatrix}$ Ⓓ $\begin{pmatrix} 0 & 3 \\ 0 & 2 \end{pmatrix}$ Ⓔ $\begin{pmatrix} -4 & -8 \\ 3 & 6 \end{pmatrix}$

19. The characteristic polynomial of $A = \begin{pmatrix} 8 & -2 & 2 \\ -2 & 5 & 4 \\ 2 & 4 & 5 \end{pmatrix}$ is $p(\lambda) = -\lambda(\lambda - 9)^2$. $\begin{pmatrix} 1 \\ 2 \\ -2 \end{pmatrix}$ is an eigenvector for 0, and $\begin{pmatrix} -2 \\ 1 \\ 0 \end{pmatrix}$ is an eigenvector for 9. Select the vector below which is another eigenvector for 9, and is also orthogonal to $\begin{pmatrix} -2 \\ 1 \\ 0 \end{pmatrix}$.

(A) $\begin{pmatrix} 0 \\ 0 \\ 9 \end{pmatrix}$ (B) $\begin{pmatrix} 2 \\ 4 \\ 3 \end{pmatrix}$ (C) $\begin{pmatrix} 4 \\ 8 \\ 2 \end{pmatrix}$ (D) $\begin{pmatrix} 3 \\ 6 \\ -1 \end{pmatrix}$ (E) $\begin{pmatrix} 2 \\ 4 \\ 5 \end{pmatrix}$

20. Let $\mathbf{F} = (x - y)\mathbf{i} - 2xz\mathbf{j} - x^2\mathbf{k}$. Evaluate

$$\iint_{\mathcal{S}} (\nabla \times \mathbf{F}) \cdot \mathbf{n} \, dS = \iint_{\mathcal{S}} (\nabla \times \mathbf{F}) \cdot d\mathbf{S},$$

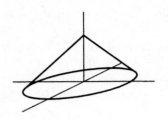

where $\mathcal{S}$ is the portion of the cone $z = 1 - \sqrt{x^2 + y^2}$ above the xy-plane with outward directed normal (away from the origin).

Equivalently, evaluate $\iint_{\mathcal{S}} P \, dy \, dz + Q \, dz \, dx + R \, dx \, dy$ where $\nabla \times \mathbf{F} = P\mathbf{i} + Q\mathbf{j} + R\mathbf{k}$.

(A) 0   (B) π (C) 2π (D) 3π (E) 4π

21. Evaluate the integral

$$\iint_{\mathcal{R}} xy \, dA$$

over the region bounded by the curves $xy = 1$, $xy = 5$, $y = x^2$ and $y = 4x^2$.

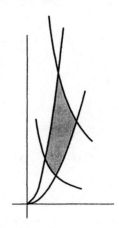

(A) $2 \ln 2$ (B) $4 \ln 2$ (C) $8 \ln 2$

(D) $12 \ln 2$ (E) $15 \ln 2$

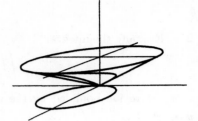

22. Find the surface area of the portion of the cone $z = \frac{1}{2}\sqrt{x^2 + y^2}$ lying above the circle $(x-1)^2 + y^2 = 1$.

(A) $\frac{4}{3}\pi$ (B) $\pi \ln 3$ (C) $\frac{\sqrt{5}}{2}\pi$

(D) $2\pi - 3$ (E) $\pi + 1$

Math 240, FINAL EXAM
December 14, 2006

INSTRUCTIONS:

1. Please complete the information requested below and on the second page of this exam. There are 15 multiple choice problems. No partial credit will be given.

2. You must show all your work on the exam itself. Blind guessing will not be credited. An answer with no supporting work may receive no credit even if correct.

3. For each problem which you want graded, transfer your answer to the answer sheet *on the second page of the exam*. We will not grade problems for which answers have not been marked on the answer sheet. Do NOT detach the answer sheet from the rest of the exam.

4. You are allowed to use one hand-written sheet of paper with formulas. NO CALCULATORS, BOOKS OR OTHER AIDS ARE ALLOWED.

- **Name** (please print):

- **Name of your professor:**

    ◯ **Dr. Kadison**   ◯ **Dr. Pantev**   ◯ **Dr. Shatz**

- **Signature:**

- **Last 4 digits of student ID number:**

- **Recitation day and time:**

1

NAME (please print):

ANSWERS TO BE GRADED

1. A ◯   B ◯   C ◯   D ◯   E ◯   F ◯

2. A ◯   B ◯   C ◯   D ◯   E ◯   F ◯

3. A ◯   B ◯   C ◯   D ◯   E ◯   F ◯

4. A ◯   B ◯   C ◯   D ◯   E ◯   F ◯

5. A ◯   B ◯   C ◯   D ◯   E ◯   F ◯

6. A ◯   B ◯   C ◯   D ◯   E ◯   F ◯

7. A ◯   B ◯   C ◯   D ◯   E ◯   F ◯

8. A ◯   B ◯   C ◯   D ◯   E ◯   F ◯

9. A ◯   B ◯   C ◯   D ◯   E ◯   F ◯

10. A ◯   B ◯   C ◯   D ◯   E ◯   F ◯

11. A ◯   B ◯   C ◯   D ◯   E ◯   F ◯

12. A ◯   B ◯   C ◯   D ◯   E ◯   F ◯

13. A ◯   B ◯   C ◯   D ◯   E ◯   F ◯

14. A ◯   B ◯   C ◯   D ◯   E ◯   F ◯

15. A ◯   B ◯   C ◯   D ◯   E ◯   F ◯

(1) For which real values of c is the matrix $A = \begin{pmatrix} c & 1 \\ c^2 - 1 & c \end{pmatrix}$ diagonalizable as a real matrix?

(**A**) $c = \pm 1$ (**B**) $-1 < c < 1$ (**C**) $c \le -1$
(**D**) $c \ge 1$ (**E**) $|c| > 1$ (**F**) $c = -1$

3

(2) For the matrix A and the vector of unknowns $\vec{x}$ given by

$$A = \begin{pmatrix} 1 & -1 & -1 & -1 & 2 & 3 \\ 2 & 8 & -1 & 1 & 2 & 0 \\ 5 & 5 & -4 & -2 & 8 & 9 \\ 1 & 9 & 0 & 2 & 0 & -3 \end{pmatrix}, \qquad \vec{x} = \begin{pmatrix} x_1 \\ x_2 \\ x_3 \\ x_4 \\ x_5 \\ x_6 \end{pmatrix}$$

we have

(A) rank$(A) = 1$ and the solutions of the homogeneous linear system $A\vec{x} = \vec{0}$ depend on 3 parameters.

(B) rank$(A) = 2$ and the solutions of the homogeneous linear system $A\vec{x} = \vec{0}$ depend on 2 parameters.

(C) rank$(A) = 3$ and the solutions of the homogeneous linear system $A\vec{x} = \vec{0}$ depend on 3 parameters.

(D) rank$(A) = 2$ and the solutions of the homogeneous linear system $A\vec{x} = \vec{0}$ depend on 4 parameters.

(E) rank$(A) = 1$ and the solutions of the homogeneous linear system $A\vec{x} = \vec{0}$ depend on 5 parameters.

(F) rank$(A) = 3$ and the solutins of the homogeneous linear system $A\vec{x} = \vec{0}$ depend on 2 parameters.

4

(3) Which of the following statements is *false*:

(A) If A is an 3×3 matrix with real entries, and the only solution of the system $A\vec{x} = \vec{0}$ is the zero vector, then A is invertible.

(B) There exists a 2×2 matrix A so that $A \begin{pmatrix} 1 \\ 2 \end{pmatrix} = \begin{pmatrix} 4 \\ 8 \end{pmatrix}$ and $A \begin{pmatrix} 1 \\ 1 \end{pmatrix} = \begin{pmatrix} 2 \\ 2 \end{pmatrix}$.

(C) If A and B are diagonalizable 3×3 matrices with the same eigenvectors, then $A + B$ is diagonalizable.

(D) There exists a real 3×3 matrix A which satisfies $A^4 = -I_3$.

(E) An $n \times n$ real matrix can have at most n real eigenvalues.

(F) If $\vec{v} = \begin{pmatrix} 3 \\ 0 \\ -4 \end{pmatrix}$, then the matrix $A = \vec{v}\,\vec{v}^T$ has three linearly independent eigenvectors.

5

(4) Consider the matrix
$$B = \begin{pmatrix} 0 & 0 & -2 \\ 1 & 0 & 1 \\ 0 & 1 & 2 \end{pmatrix}.$$
It is known that 2 is an eigenvalue of B. Then

(A) B is diagonalizable with eigenvalues 1, 1, and 2.

(B) B is diagonalizable with eigenvalues 1, 2, and 2.

(C) B is diagonalizable with eigenvalues -1, 1, and 2.

(D) B is not diagonalizable, and has eigenvalues -1, 1, and 2.

(E) B is not diagonalizable, and has eigenvalues 1, 1, and 2.

(F) B is not diagonalizable, and has a unique real eigenvalue 2.

6

(5) A surface Σ is given by the equation $z = x^2 + 2y$ Find the unit normal vector to Σ at the point $(0, 1, 2)$

(A) $\dfrac{2}{\sqrt{5}}\,\widehat{\imath} + \dfrac{1}{\sqrt{5}}\,\widehat{k}$ (B) $\dfrac{-2}{\sqrt{5}}\,\widehat{\jmath} + \dfrac{1}{\sqrt{5}}\,\widehat{k}$ (C) $\dfrac{2}{\sqrt{5}}\,\widehat{\jmath} + \dfrac{1}{\sqrt{5}}\,\widehat{k}$

(D) $\dfrac{-1}{\sqrt{5}}\,\widehat{\imath} + \dfrac{2}{\sqrt{5}}\,\widehat{k}$ (E) $\dfrac{1}{\sqrt{5}}\,\widehat{\imath} + \dfrac{-2}{\sqrt{5}}\,\widehat{\jmath}$ (F) $\dfrac{1}{\sqrt{5}}\,\widehat{\jmath} + \dfrac{-2}{\sqrt{5}}\,\widehat{k}$

(6) Let
$$\vec{F} = (xz + 2e^{yz})\,\hat{\imath} + x^2 z\,\hat{\jmath} + \left(\cos^2 y - z\right)\,\hat{k},$$

and let S be the sphere of radius 5 centered at the origin. Evaluate $\iint_S \vec{F} \cdot \vec{n}\, dS$, where $\vec{n}$ is the outward unit normal.

(A) 125π (B) -25π (C) 0

(D) $\dfrac{125\pi}{3}$ (E) $-\dfrac{25\pi}{3}$ (F) $-\dfrac{500\pi}{3}$

8

(7) Evaluate the line integral

$$\int_C (e^x \sin y - 5y)\, dx + (e^x \cos y - 5)\, dy,$$

where C is the semicircle $x^2 + y^2 = 2x$, $y \geq 0$, centered at $(1,0)$ and oriented counterclockwise from $(2,0)$ to $(0,0)$.

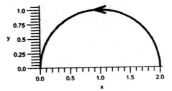

(A) 0   (B) $-e^\pi$ (C) $e^\pi - 10$

(D) $\dfrac{5\pi}{2}$ (E) $\dfrac{\pi}{2}$ (F) $-\dfrac{3\pi}{2} - 10$

9

(8) Let C be the curve parameterized by $\vec{r}(t) = t\hat{\imath} + \sin(t)\hat{\jmath} + t^2\cos(t)\,\hat{k}$, for $0 \le t \le \pi$, and let $f(x,y,z) = z^2 e^{\sin(x)} + y^2\cos(x)$. Compute the line integral $\int_C \vec{\nabla}f \cdot d\vec{r}$ of the gradient vector field $\vec{\nabla}f$ of f.

(A) 0   (B) $-\pi$ (C) e

(D) π^4 (E) $e - \pi$ (F) none of the above

(9) Let $y(x)$ be the general solution of the linear differential equation

$$x^2 y'' + 5xy' + 3y = 0,$$

for which $y(1) = 1$ and $y'(1) = -3$. Find $y(1/2)$.

(A) -9 (B) 2   (C) 0

(D) 1/8   (E) 8   (F) 1/16

(10) The differential equation $xy' - y = 100$, $x > 0$ has a unique solution for which $y(1) = 50$. Find $y(3)$

(A) 250   (B) 300   (C) 350
(D) 400   (E) 450   (F) 500

12

(11) Consider the differential equation

$$y''' - y' - y = t.$$

Then the solution $y(t)$ for which $y(0) = 0$, $y'(0) = 1$, $y''(0) = 1$ has Laplace transform

(A) $\dfrac{s^3 + s^2 + 1}{s^2(s^3 - s - 1)}$ (B) $\dfrac{s^3 - s - 1}{s(s^3 + s^2 + 1)}$ (C) $\dfrac{s^3 - s - 1}{s^2(s^3 + s^2 + 1)}$

(D) $\dfrac{s^3 + s^2 + 1}{s(s^3 - s - 1)}$ (E) $\dfrac{s^3 + s + 1}{s(s^3 - s - 1)}$ (F) $\dfrac{s^2 + s + 1}{s^2(s^3 - s - 1)}$

13

(12) Let $Y(s)$ be the Laplace transform of the function $y(t)$. Find the Laplace transform of the spring-mass equation with damping and sharp impulse function,

$$y'' + 2y' + y = \delta(t - 1), \quad y(0) = 1, \ y'(0) = -1$$

(A) $s^2 Y(s) - s - 1 + 2sY(s) + Y(s) = \mathcal{U}(t - 1).$

(B) $s^2 Y(s) - s - 1 + 2sY(s) + Y(s) = e^{-s}.$

(C) $s^2 Y(s) + s - 3 + 2sY(s) + Y(s) = e^{-s}.$

(D) $s^{-2} Y(s) + s^{-1} + 3 + 2s^{-1}Y(s) + Y(s) = s^{-1}.$

(E) $4Y(s) - 3s - s^2 = e^s.$

(F) $4sY(s) - 3s - s^2 = e^s.$

(13) Consider the differential equation

$$x^2 y'' + 2x(x+1)y' - y = 0.$$

It has a Frobenius power series solution $y(x) = x^\alpha \sum_{j=0}^{\infty} a_j x^j$ for

(A) $\alpha = \pm\dfrac{1}{2}$ (B) $\alpha = \pm\dfrac{\sqrt{3}}{2}$ (C) $\alpha = 0$ and $\alpha = \dfrac{\sqrt{5}}{2}$

(D) $\alpha = -\dfrac{1}{2} \pm \dfrac{\sqrt{3}}{2}$ (E) $\alpha = -\dfrac{1}{2} \pm \dfrac{\sqrt{5}}{2}$ (F) $\alpha = \dfrac{1}{2}$ and $\alpha = \dfrac{\sqrt{5}}{2}$

(14) Find the recursion formula for the coefficients of the power series solution $y(x) = \sum_{n=0}^{+\infty} c_n x^n$ about the ordinary point $x = 0$ of the differential equation,

$$y'' + 2xy' + 2y = 0$$

(A) $c_{n+2} = \dfrac{-c_n}{n+2}$ (B) $c_{n+2} = \dfrac{c_{n-1}}{n+1}$ (C) $c_{n+2} = \dfrac{-3c_n}{n+1}$

(D) $c_{n+1} = c_n$ (E) $c_{n+2} = \dfrac{-3c_n + 1}{n+1}$ (F) $c_{n+2} = \dfrac{-2c_n}{n+2}$

16

(15) Solve the system of first-order linear differential equations with initial value,

$$\frac{dx}{dt} = -4x + 2y,$$
$$\frac{dy}{dt} = 2x - 4y,$$

$$\begin{pmatrix} x(0) \\ y(0) \end{pmatrix} = \begin{pmatrix} 1 \\ -1 \end{pmatrix}$$

(A) $\begin{pmatrix} 0 \\ 1 \end{pmatrix} e^{-6t} + \begin{pmatrix} 1 \\ -2 \end{pmatrix} e^{-2t}$ (B) $\begin{pmatrix} 1 \\ -1 \end{pmatrix} e^{-6t} + \begin{pmatrix} 1 \\ 1 \end{pmatrix} e^{-2t}$

(C) $\begin{pmatrix} 1 \\ -2 \end{pmatrix} e^{6t} + \begin{pmatrix} 0 \\ 1 \end{pmatrix} e^{2t}$ (D) $\begin{pmatrix} 1 \\ -1 \end{pmatrix} e^{-6t}$

(E) $\begin{pmatrix} 1 \\ -1 \end{pmatrix} e^{-2t}$ (F) $\begin{pmatrix} 1 \\ 1 \end{pmatrix} e^{-2t}$

17

Mathematics Department

University *of* Pennsylvania

Final Exam, Math 240: Calculus III

May 3, 2007

No calculators books and notes can be used, other than a two-sided handwritten A4 sheet of paper.

- Name:

- Penn Id (last 4 of the middle 8 digits):

- Instructor:

◯ Dr. Rimmer   ◯ Dr. Temkin   ◯ Dr. Katzarkov

The duration of the exam is 2 hours. There are seven free response questions which worth 10 points and eight multiple choice questions which worth 5 points. Thus, the total number of points is 110, and each grade above 100 will be cut to 100. Show your work in the space provided after each question and **circle your answer** in the multiple choice questions. No part credit is given in the multiple choice part of this exam, but you must show your work: blind guessing will not be credited. Part credit may be given for free response part, so be sure to show all details of your solution. Good luck!

1	2	3	4	5	6	7	8	9	10	11	12	13	14	15

total

1. (10 points) Let A and B be real $n \times n$ matrix. Decide whether each of the following statements is true or false, you do not need to justify your answer.

(i) (3 points) Always $A^T B^T = (AB)^T$.

(ii) (3 points) If A and B are invertible then always $B^{-1} A^{-1} = (AB)^{-1}$.

(iii) (4 points) If A is diagonalizable then it has n distinct eigenvalues.

(i)	a) true	b) false
(ii)	a) true	b) false
(iii)	a) true	b) false

2. (10 points) Show that if a real 3×3 matrix A satisfies $A^T = -A$, then its rank is smaller than 3.

3. (10 points) Given a matrix

$$A = \begin{pmatrix} -2 & 1 & 1 \\ 1 & -2 & 1 \\ 1 & 1 & -2 \end{pmatrix}$$

find its diagonalization, i.e. find an invertible matrix P and a diagonal matrix D so that $P^{-1}AP = D$.

P=

D=

4. (10 points) Decide whether each of the following statements is true or false, you do not need to justify your answer.

(i) (3 points) If y_1 and y_2 are two solutions of the differential equation $e^x y'' + \sin(x)y' + \cos(x)y = 0$, then $y_1 - y_2$ is also a solution.

(ii) (3 points) If line integrals $\int_C Pdx + Qdy$ are independent of path in $\mathbf{R}^2$, then $Pdx + Qdy$ is an exact differential, i.e. $Pdx + Qdy = d\Phi$ for some function Φ on $\mathbf{R}^2$.

(iii) (4 points) If X is an open ball in $\mathbf{R}^3$, a vector field $\mathbf{F}$ on X has continuous partial derivatives and $\mathrm{curl}(\mathbf{F}) = 0$, then $\mathbf{F}$ is potential, i.e. $\mathbf{F} = \mathrm{grad}(\Phi)$ for some function $\Phi(x, y, z)$ on X.

(i)	a) true	b) false
(ii)	a) true	b) false
(iii)	a) true	b) false

5. (10 points) Solve the differential equation $y'' - 2xy = 0$ by a power series expansion about $x = 0$. You are done when you have written out the recurrence relation for the coefficients and the first three **non-zero** terms of two linearly independent solutions y_1 and y_2.

coefficient recurrence:_____

$y_1 =$_____

$y_2 =$_____

6. (10 points) Find the solution of the system of linear first order differential equations $\mathbf{Y}' = A\mathbf{Y}$ that satisfies the initial condition $\mathbf{Y}(0) = \mathbf{a}_0$, where

$$A = \begin{pmatrix} 3 & 4 \\ 2 & 1 \end{pmatrix}, \mathbf{Y} = \begin{pmatrix} y_1 \\ y_2 \end{pmatrix}, \mathbf{a}_0 = \begin{pmatrix} 16 \\ -1 \end{pmatrix}$$

$y_1 = $ _____

$y_2 = $ _____

7. (10 points) Use **Laplace transform** to solve the initial value problem $y' + 3y = \sin t$, $y(0) = 1$.

$y = \underline{\hspace{4cm}}$

8. (5 points) Solve the system of linear equations

$$\begin{cases} 3x + y + z = -3 \\ 2x + 3z = 2 \\ -2x - 3y + z = 3 \end{cases}$$

Then x equals to
a) 1;   b) 0;   c) 3;   d) -1;
e) -3;   f) 4;   g) -2;   h) 2.

9. (5 points) Find $\det(A^{-1}BA^{T})$, where

$$A = \begin{pmatrix} 3 & 2 & 1 \\ 5 & 4 & 0 \\ 6 & 0 & 0 \end{pmatrix}, B = \begin{pmatrix} 1 & 2 & 3 \\ 8 & 0 & 4 \\ 7 & 6 & 5 \end{pmatrix}$$

a) 120;　　b) 144;　　c) 24;　　d) -120;

e) -144;　　f) 96;　　g) -24;　　h) -96.

10. (5 points) Let C be the arc of the parabola $x = t, y = 2 - t - t^2$ given by $-2 \le t \le 1$, and $\mathbf{F} = 2xe^{x^2-1}\cos(y)\mathbf{i} - e^{x^2-1}\sin(y)\mathbf{j}$ be a vector field. Evaluate the line integral

$$\int_C \mathbf{F} \cdot d\mathbf{r}$$

a) $\frac{e+e^{-1}}{2}$;   b) $\frac{e^2+e^{-2}}{2}$;   c) $e^3 - e^{-1}$;   d) $\frac{e-e^{-1}}{2}$;

e) 1;   f) 0;   g) $1 - e^3$;   h) $e^3 - 1$.

11. (5 points) Let C denote the circumference $(x-2)^2 + (y-2)^2 = 1$ traversed counterclockwise. Evaluate the line integral

$$\oint_C (x^6 + 3y)dx + (2x - e^{y^2})dy$$

a) 0;   b) e^4;   c) $-\pi$;   d) -2π;

e) 2π;   f) π;   g) $-e^4$;   h) $\pi - e^4$.

12. (5 points) Let S be the portion of the cone $z = 1 - \sqrt{x^2 + y^2}$ lying above the xy-plane. We orient S by a unit upward normal $\mathbf{n}$. Given a vector field $\mathbf{F} = y\mathbf{i} + \sin(z^2)\mathbf{j} + \cos(x^2)\mathbf{k}$, evaluate the surface integral

$$\iint_S \mathrm{curl}(\mathbf{F}) \cdot \mathbf{n}\, dS$$

a) $\sin(\pi^2)$;   b) π;   c) $-\pi$;   d) -2π;

e) $\cos(\pi^2) - \sin(\pi^2)$;   f) 2π;   g) $-\sin(\pi^2)$;   h) 0.

13. (5 points) Let S be the sphere $x^2 + y^2 + z^2 = 4$ oriented by the outward unit normal $\mathbf{n} = \frac{1}{2}(x\mathbf{i} + y\mathbf{j} + z\mathbf{k})$ and

$$\mathbf{F} = (xy + x)\mathbf{i} + (y - y^2)\mathbf{j} + (yz + z)\mathbf{k}$$

be a vector field. Evaluate the surface integral

$$\iint_S \mathbf{F} \cdot \mathbf{n}\, dS$$

a) -32π;   b) 32π;   c) -8π;   d) 16π;

e) $\frac{16\pi}{3}$;   f) 8π;   g) -16π;   h) 0.

14. (5 points) Solve the initial value problem $2y'' + 2y' + y = x + 2$, $y(0) = 1$, $y'(0) = 0$. Then $y(\pi)$ equals to

   a) $\pi + 2$;   b) $\pi + e^{-\frac{\pi}{2}}$;   c) $e^{-\pi}$;   d) $\pi + \frac{e^{-\pi}}{2}$;

   e) $-e^{-\frac{\pi}{2}}$;   f) $\pi - e^{-\pi}$;   g) $2e^{-\pi}$;   h) $\pi - e^{-\frac{\pi}{2}}$.

16

15. (5 points) A linear differential equation
$$3x^2y'' + (x - x^2)y' + (x - 1)y = 0$$
has solutions $y_1 = x^{r_1}(1 + c_1 x + c_2 x^2 + \dots)$ and $y_2 = x^{r_2}(1 + d_1 x + d_2 x^2 + \dots)$ about $x = 0$. Find r_1 and r_2.

a) $r_1 = 0, r_2 = 1$;

b) $r_1 = -1, r_2 = 3$;

c) $r_1 = \frac{1-\sqrt{13}}{6}, r_2 = \frac{1+\sqrt{13}}{6}$;

d) $r_1 = 0, r_2 = \frac{1}{3}$;

e) $r_1 = -\frac{1}{3}, r_2 = 1$;

f) $r_1 = \frac{3-\sqrt{21}}{2}, r_2 = \frac{3+\sqrt{21}}{2}$;

g) $r_1 = \frac{1-\sqrt{13}}{2}, r_2 = \frac{1+\sqrt{13}}{2}$;

h) $r_1 = \frac{3-\sqrt{21}}{6}, r_2 = \frac{3+\sqrt{21}}{6}$.

Math240, Spring 2007

Answer Key

1. (i) false, (ii) true, (iii) false.

2. Solution is not unique, a possible solution is as follows. Since $\det(A^T) = \det(A)$, we obtain that $\det(A) = \det(-A) = (-1)^3 \det(A) = -\det(A)$. So, $\det(A) = 0$, and therefore A is singular and its rank is smaller than 3.

3. Answer is not unique, a possible answer is

$$P = \begin{pmatrix} 1 & 1 & 1 \\ 1 & -1 & 0 \\ 1 & 0 & -1 \end{pmatrix}, \quad D = \begin{pmatrix} 0 & 0 & 0 \\ 0 & -3 & 0 \\ 0 & 0 & -3 \end{pmatrix}.$$

4. (i) true, (ii) true, (iii) true.

5. $c_2 = 0$ and $c_{n+3} = \frac{2}{(n+3)(n+2)} c_n$ for $n \geq 0$; a possible choice of y's is as follows: $y_1 = 1 + \frac{1}{3}x^3 + \frac{1}{45}x^6 + \ldots$ and $y_2 = x + \frac{1}{6}x^4 + \frac{1}{126}x^7 + \ldots$ (a more tricky choice is to take, for example, $y_1 = 1 + x + \frac{1}{3}x^3 + \ldots$ and $y_2 = 1 - x + \frac{1}{3}x^3 + \ldots$).

6. $y_1 = 10e^{5t} + 6e^{-t}, y_2 = 5e^{5t} - 6e^{-t}$.

7. $y = \left(11e^{-3t} + 3\sin(t) - \cos(t)\right)/10$.

8. (g)

9. (f)

10. (g)

11. (c)

12. (c)

13. (b)

14. (h)

15. (e)

MATHEMATICS 240   **J. KRIEGER, N. RIMMER, S. SHATZ**
FINAL EXAMINATION   **DECEMBER 12, 2007**   **9:00 AM**

Answer all questions by circling the **entire** statement you deem correct in each question. No books, tables, notes, calculators, computers or cell phones allowed. You may bring one 8.5" x 11" sheet of paper bearing any handwritten material you deem necessary and you may use both sides of this paper. **No partial credit.** Use the backs of your exam pages for scratch work and calculations.

---   ---------------------------------
(Your name—please print)   **(Your PENN ID number)**

---   ---------------------------------
(Your signature)   **(Your instructor's name (print))**

PLEASE DO NOT WRITE BELOW THIS LINE

PROBLEM	SCORE	PROBLEM	SCORE	PROBLEM	SCORE
I		VI		XI	
II		VII		XII	
III		VIII		XIII	
IV		IX		XIV	
V		X		XV	

TOTAL-----------------

I)   For the differential equation

$$y'' - x^2 y' + xy = 0$$

and the solution, $y(x)$, determined by the initial conditions $y(0) = 0$ and $y'(0) = 1$, when we write $y(x)$ in a power series, the coefficient of x^4 in this series is:

a) -1/24   b) 1/2   c) -1/6   d) 2/3   e) 0

II)   Given the vectors: $(1, t, -1)$; $(0, 1, -2)$; $(1, (s + 2), -s)$, find the condition on t and s so that these vectors are linearly dependent.

a) $s = 2t + 5$ b) $s = 2t - 5$ c) $t - s = 5$

d) $t + s = 5$ e) none of these

III)   An iron bead is constrained to move along the x-axis and is acted on by a varying magnetic field. The differential equation describing its motion is:

$$x'' + (1/2)\, x' + 2x = \cos(t).$$

Suppose $x(0) = 4/5$ and $x'(0) = 2/5$, then $x(3\pi/2)$ equals:

a) 4/5   b) 3/5   c) -2/5   d) 2/5   e) -4/5

IV)   Suppose A and B are 3 x 3 matrices and det $A = x \neq 0$ while det $B = y$. Let C be the matrix $(2A)^{-1}B$, then det C is:

a) y/8x   b) 2xy   c) -2y/x   d) 2y/x   e) 8y/x

-- page 3

(Your name)

V)   Given a 4 x 4 matrix, M, we form the augmented 4 x 8 matrix $Y = (M \mid I)$ and row reduce Y to row reduced echelon form. When this is done we get the new matrix

$$\tilde{Y} = \begin{matrix} 1 & 0 & 0 & 0 \\ 0 & 1 & 0 & 0 \\ 0 & 0 & 1 & 0 \\ 0 & 0 & 0 & 0 \end{matrix}$$

If $X = (x_1, x_2, x_3, x_4)$ and $b = (b_1, b_2, b_3, b_4)$, where the x_i are unknowns and the b_i are given numbers and each of X and b is viewed as a column vector, then we consider the matrix equation $MX = b$ and for it we can say:

a) For each b there is a unique solution, but it may not be Cb.

b) There are vectors b for which there is no solution.

c) For each given b there are always many solutions.

d) For each b there is a unique solution; it is Cb.

e) Need more information about M and b to decide among the above choices.

VI)   Evaluate the line integral $\int_C \mathbf{F} \cdot d\mathbf{r}$ in which C is the curve $\mathbf{r}(t) = (t, t^2, t^3)$ for $0 \le t \le 1$ and $\mathbf{F}$ is the vector field $(e^y, xe^y, (z+1)e^z)$.

a) 1/2   b) 2e   c) 0   d) e   e) e/2

VII)   Recall that for a matrix its trace is the sum of its eigenvalues and its determinant is the product of its eigenvalues. Which of the following is **false**?

a) There is a symmetric 3x3 matrix with an eigenvalue 2, trace 5 and det = 4.

b) For any 3 x 3 matrix, A, the matrix $A(A^T)$ is always diagonalizable.

c) Symmetric matrices always have an orthonormal basis of eigenvectors.

d) There is a symmetric 3x3 matrix with an eigenvalue 2, trace 5 and det = 6.

e) None of the above.

(Your name)

VIII)   Consider the region Ω whose boundary consists of **two** curves: $x^2 + y^2 = 4$ and $x^2 + y^2 = \frac{1}{2}$ oriented and labeled as shown in the sketch below. Write C for the boundary of Ω and let **F** be the vector field

$$\mathbf{F}(x, y) = (-y/[(x-1)^2 + y^2],\ (x-1)/[(x-1)^2 + y^2]).$$

Then $\int_C \mathbf{F} \cdot d\mathbf{r}$ equals:

a) 2π b) -4π c) 4π d) 0 e) -2π

IX)   When we solve the differential equation

$$x^2(2 + x)y'' + 2xy' - 3y = 0$$

by the Frobenius method, the exponents, r, in the solution $y = x^r \sum c_i x^i$ are:

a) $r = \pm 2$ b) $r = -1 \pm \sqrt{3}$ c) $r = \pm\sqrt{3}$ d) $r = \pm\sqrt{(3/2)}$ e) $r = \pm 1$

X)   Evaluate the line integral $\int_C (y + e^{\sqrt{x}})dx + (2x - \cos(y^2))dy$, where C is the boundary of the region enclosed between the curves $y = x^2$ and $x = y^2$ and C is oriented counter-clockwise.

a) $1/3$ b) 3 c) 0 d) $\pi/3$ e) π

(Your name)

XI)   Suppose A is the 3 x 3 matrix:

$$\begin{array}{ccc} 1 & 1 & 0 \\ 0 & 1 & 0 \\ 0 & -1 & 2 \end{array}$$

Then

a) A has eigenvalues 1, 1, 2 and is not diagonalizable.

b) A has eigenvalues 0, 1, 2 and is not diagonalizable.

c) A has eigenvalues 1, 1, 2 and is diagonalizable.

d) A has eigenvalues 0, 1, 2 and is diagonalizable.

e) None of the above.

XII)   For the initial value problem:

$$y'' - 3y' + 2y = U(t-1)\,; \; y(0) = 0, \; y'(0) = 1,$$

in which U(t) is the function that is 0 when $t < 0$ and 1 when $t \ge 0$, the Laplace transform of y, namely $L(y)(s)$, is given by

a) $1/(s^2 - 3s + 2) + e^{-s}/(s(s^2 - 3s + 2))$ b) $1/(s^2 - 3s + 2) - e^{-s}/(s(s^2 - 3s + 2))$

c) $1/(s^2 - 3s + 2)$ d) $1/s(s^2 - 3s + 2)$

e) Cannot be determined

(Your name)

XIII)　　　Consider the surface, S, formed by the upper half of the ellipsoid

$$x^2 + y^2 + 6z^2 = 1,$$

and write C for the circle $x^2 + y^2 = 1$ where S cuts the xy-plane. We use the outer normal (upward pointing) to orient S so that C is traversed counter-clockwise in the xy-plane (when viewed from above). Let **F** be the vector field

$$(\sin(xz) + \sqrt{z}, \ (3 + z)x - e^y, \ x^2 - y^3 - z^5)$$

Compute the surface integral $\iint_S$ **curl F · n** dS:

a) $-\pi$　　　　b) π　　　　c) -3π　　　　d) 3π　　　　e) none of these

XIV)　　　We solve the differential equation $y'' + (t - (t^3/6))y = 0$ by a series $\sum a_i t^i$ and assume the initial conditions $y(0) = y'(0) = 1$.
Then the expression

$$(a_2)^3 + (a_3)^2 - a_4$$

equals:

a) $-1/3$　　　　b) $1/9$　　　　c) $1/12$　　　　d) $-1/12$　　　　e) $1/6$

XV)　　　Write S for the part of the surface $z = x^2 + y^2$ over the disc $x^2 + y^2 \leq 1$ in the plane. We orient S so that its normal, **n**, points downward. If the vector field, **F**, is given by: $\mathbf{F}(x, y, z) = (e^y + x, \ e^{\sin(z)} + \sin(x), \ -z + xy)$, then the surface integral $\iint_S$ **F · n** dS equals:

a) 2π　　　　b) 4π　　　　c) π　　　　d) $\pi/2$　　　　e) None of these.

(END OF THE EXAM)

Final Exam - April 29, 2005
Math 241

Name:_____

Instructor:_____

TA and Recitation:_____

No calculators, books or notes are allowed. You may use two $8.5'' \times 11''$ two-sided pages of crib sheets, which must be turned in with your exam. Show your work in the space provided for each problem, or in the back of the corresponding page, or in one of the blank pages provided in the back of the exam.

Make sure to show all your work, clearly and in order, if you want to get full credit. We reserve the right to take off points if we cannot see how you arrived at your answer (even if your final answer is correct). Good luck!

Question	Points
1	/10
2	/10
3	/10
4	/10
5	/10
6	/10
7	/10
8	/14
9	/16
TOTAL	/100

1. TRUE or FALSE.

(a) The radius of convergence of the Taylor series of $f(z) = \dfrac{\sin z}{(z+2)^2}$ around $z = 1$ is $R=1$.

(b) Let C_1 be the positively oriented circle of radius 2 and let C_2 be the positively oriented circle of radius 5. Then

$$\oint_{C_1} \left[\frac{1}{z+1} + \frac{1}{z-4} \right] dz = \oint_{C_2} \left[\frac{1}{z+1} + \frac{1}{z-4} \right] dz$$

2. **(I)** If $f(x) = x^2 - x$ is expanded in a Fourier series on the interval $[-2, 2]$, then at $x = 2$ the series will converge to

   (a) 0

   (b) 1

   (b) 2

   (c) 3

   (d) 4

   (e) 5

   (f) 6

   (II) What is the image of the line $x = 1$ under the map $f(z) = e^z$?

   (a) A circle

   (b) A horizontal line

   (c) A vertical line

   (d) A hyperbola

   (e) A logarithmic spiral

   (f) None of these

3. Compute the complex Fourier series for $f(x) = \begin{cases} 3, & |x| < 1 \\ 0, & |x| > 1 \end{cases}$ which is valid on the interval $(-2, 2)$.

4. Using separation of variables find the solution of

$$\frac{\partial^2 u}{\partial t^2} - 2\frac{\partial u}{\partial t} = \frac{\partial^2 u}{\partial x^2}$$

satisfying

$$u(0,t) = 0, \qquad\qquad u\left(\frac{\pi}{2}, t\right) = 0,$$
$$u(x,0) = 0, \qquad\qquad u_t(x,0) = f(x)$$

Express the coefficients of the solution in terms of $f(x)$.

5. Find the steady-state temperature in a semicircular metal plate of radius 2, if the round part is held at a temperature of 100 degrees and the flat bottom part is held at 0 degrees.

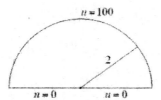

6. Using a Fourier Transform find the steady-state temperature $u(x, y)$ on the semi-infinite plate satisfying

$$u_{xx} + u_{yy} = 0, \qquad 0 < x < \pi, y > 0$$
$$u_y(x, 0) = 0, \qquad 0 < x < \pi$$
$$u(0, y) = 0, \qquad u(\pi, y) = \begin{cases} 1 & y < 1 \\ 0 & y > 1 \end{cases}$$

Express your final answer as an inverse Fourier transform integral.

7. Find the Laurent series of $f(z) = \dfrac{2z}{z^2 - 2z - 8}$ valid for $|z + 2| > 6$.

8. Classify the singularity of each of the following functions at $z_0 = 0$ and find the corresponding residue.

(a) $f(z) = \dfrac{1}{z(e^z - 1)}$ Type: Residue=

(b) $f(z) = z^3 e^{-1/z^2}$ Type: Residue=

9. Compute the following integrals:

(a) $\displaystyle\int_0^{2\pi} \frac{1}{5 + 4\cos\theta}\, d\theta$

(b) $\displaystyle\int_{-\infty}^{\infty} \frac{\cos x}{(x^2 + 4)(x^2 + 1)}\, dx$

Feel free to use this page for scratch.

1. Find the Fourier series for the function $f(x) = \begin{cases} -1-x, & -1 < x < 0 \\ 1-x, & 0 < x < 1 \end{cases}$. Write out terms through $n = 3$.

2. Solve the one-dimensional heat equation for a laterally insulated bar of length π whose ends are held at $0°$ and across which the initial temperature distribution is given by $f(x) = \begin{cases} x, & < x < \dfrac{\pi}{2} \\ \pi - x, & \dfrac{\pi}{2} < x < \pi \end{cases}$.

3. Find *all* product solutions for $u(x, y)$ if $xu_x - yu_y = 0$.

4. Find all of the cube roots of $z = 4 + i4\sqrt{3}$. Sketch the roots iin the complex plane.

5. Which, if any of the functions listed below are analytic in the domain $z \neq 0$?

   a) $\log z$ b) $\dfrac{1}{z^2}$ c) $\dfrac{1}{e^z}$

6. Is there a function $v(x, y)$ corresponding to $u(x,y) = x^3 - y^3 + 6xy$ such that $f(z) = u(x,y) + iv(x,y)$ is an analytic complex function? If such a v exists, find it, write $f(z)$ and compute $f'(z)$.

7. Evaluate $\displaystyle\int_C z\bar{z}\, dz$ if C is the straight line from $z = 0$ to $z = 2+4i$.

8. Evaluate $\displaystyle\int_C \sin z\, dz$ where C is the semi-circle $|z| = 1$ in the upper half-plane starting at $z = 1$ and ending at $z = -1$.

9. Evaluate $\displaystyle\oint_C \frac{7z-6}{z^2 - 2z}\, dz$ where C is the ellipse $\dfrac{(x-1)^2}{9} + y^2 = 1$.

10. Find the Maclaurin series for $f(z) = \arctan(z)$ and determine the radius of convergence of your series by some suitable means. {HINT: first find a series for the derivative $f'(z) = \dfrac{1}{z^2 + 1}$ then integrate that series termwise.}

11. Write out the first four terms of the Laurent series for $f(z) = z^2 \sin\left(\dfrac{1}{z}\right)$ with center $z_0 = 0$, then:

    a) give the residue of $f(z)$ at $z = 0$;
    b) check one-- $z_0 = 0$ is   ❏ a pole of order _____ ;
                                        ❏ an essential singularity.

12.   Evaluate the contour integral $\oint_C z^3 e^{-1/z^2} dz$ where C is any circle centered at the $z = 0$ traversed in the clockwise direction.

13.   Evaluate the real integral $\int_0^{2\pi} \frac{1}{1+\cos\theta} d\theta$.

14.   Evaluate the contour integral $\oint_C \frac{e^z}{z(z^2 + \pi^2)} dz$ over each of the following (positively oriented) contours:

   a0 $|z| = 4$ b) $|z - 4i| = 2$ c) $|z - 2| = 1$

NAME: _____   **PENN ID#:** _____

(201) (202) (203) (204)   Math 241-001   Ron DONAGI/Matthew WIENER

(211) (212) (213) (214)   Math 241-002   Michael PIMSNER/Matthew WIENER

Instructions.

Please write your name and Penn ID in the space provided above, and fill in the oval identifying your recitation. You will have 2 hours to complete this exam.

You are allowed to use one $8\frac{1}{2} \times 11$ sheet, both sides, for notes you wrote yourself. In addition, an extra sheet of notes will be provided with the exam. You are not allowed to use calculators.

Do not detach this sheet from the body of the exam.

This is a multiple-choice test, but you must show your work. Blind guessing will not be credited. No penalties for incorrect answers will be taken.

Please mark your answer on both the front sheet and on the problem itself. If you change an answer, be absolutely clear which choice is your final answer.

Each problem is worth 1 point. No partial credit will be given. No penalties for incorrect answers will be taken.

	Questions 1-9						points		Questions 10-18						points
1.	(A)	(B)	(C)	(D)	(E)	(F)	1	10.	(A)	(B)	(C)	(D)	(E)	(F)	1
2.	(A)	(B)	(C)	(D)	(E)	(F)	1	11.	(A)	(B)	(C)	(D)	(E)	(F)	1
3.	(A)	(B)	(C)	(D)	(E)	(F)	1	12.	(A)	(B)	(C)	(D)	(E)	(F)	1
4.	(A)	(B)	(C)	(D)	(E)	(F)	1	13.	(A)	(B)	(C)	(D)	(E)	(F)	1
5.	(A)	(B)	(C)	(D)	(E)	(F)	1	14.	(A)	(B)	(C)	(D)	(E)	(F)	1
6.	(A)	(B)	(C)	(D)	(E)	(F)	1	15.	(A)	(B)	(C)	(D)	(E)	(F)	1
7.	(A)	(B)	(C)	(D)	(E)	(F)	1	16.	(A)	(B)	(C)	(D)	(E)	(F)	1
8.	(A)	(B)	(C)	(D)	(E)	(F)	1	17.	(A)	(B)	(C)	(D)	(E)	(F)	1
9.	(A)	(B)	(C)	(D)	(E)	(F)	1	18.	(A)	(B)	(C)	(D)	(E)	(F)	1

1. (*1 point*)   What is the radius of convergence of

$$f(z) = \frac{z^2 - 1}{z^4 + 5z^2 + 4}$$

when expanded in a Taylor series about $z = 2 + i$?

(A) 1   (B) 2   (C) $\sqrt{2}$ (D) $2\sqrt{2}$ (E) $\sqrt{5}$ (F) $\sqrt{13}$

2. (*1 point*)   Evaluate $\oint_C \dfrac{dz}{z^2 - 1}$ where C is the indicated path.

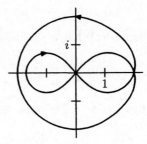

(A) 0   (B) πi (C) $2\pi i$

(D) $3\pi i$ (E) $4\pi i$ (F) $5\pi i$

3. (*1 point*)   Which region below is the image of $f(z) = e^{iz}$ when applied to the region depicted on the right, sending the light gray portion to the light gray portion, and the dark gray portion to the dark gray portion?

In all the graphs, 1 is located at the first tick mark to the right of the origin, and i is the the first tick mark above the origin.

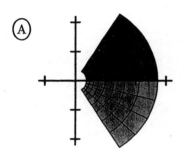

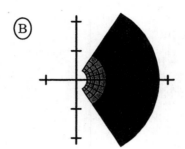

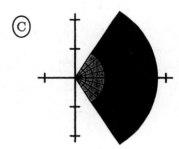

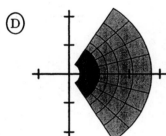

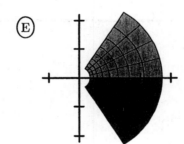

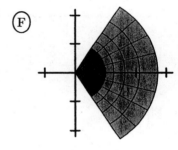

4. (*1 point*)   Solve the heat equation $u_{xx} = u_t$ with boundary conditions $u(0,t) = u(\pi,t) = 0$ for $t > 0$ and initial condition $u(x,0) = 4\sin x - 7\sin 2x + 10\sin 3x$ for $0 < x < \pi$.

(A) $4e^{-t}\sin x - 7e^{-2t}\sin 2x + 10e^{-3t}\sin 3x$

(B) $4e^{-t}\sin x - 7e^{-2t}\sin 4x + 10e^{-3t}\sin 9x$

(C) $4e^{-t}\sin x - 7e^{-4t}\sin 2x + 10e^{-9t}\sin 3x$

(D) $4e^{-t^2}\sin x - 7e^{-2t^2}\sin 2x + 10e^{-3t^2}\sin 3x$

(E) $16e^{-t}\sin x - 49e^{-4t}\sin 2x + 100e^{-9t}\sin 3x$

(F) $16e^{-t}\sin x - 49e^{-2t}\sin 2x + 100e^{-3t}\sin 3x$

5. (*1 point*)   Evaluate

$$\frac{1}{2\pi i}\oint_{|z|=1}\frac{(1+z)^{50}}{z^4}dz\,.$$

(A) 0   (B) 1   (C) 50   (D) 2^{50} (E) $50\cdot 49\cdot 48$ (F) $\dfrac{50\cdot 49\cdot 48}{1\cdot 2\cdot 3}$

6. (*1 point*)   Evaluate

$$\int_0^{2\pi} \frac{d\theta}{5 - 3\cos\theta}.$$

(A) $\frac{\pi}{4}$ (B) $\frac{\pi}{3}$ (C) $\frac{2\pi}{5}$ (D) $\frac{\pi}{2}$ (E) $\frac{4\pi}{5}$ (F) π

7. (*1 point*)   In the Laurent series expansion for $\frac{1}{z}$ centered at 1, convergent for $|z-1| > 1$, what is the coefficent of $(z-1)^{-3}$?

(A) -1 (B) $-\frac{1}{2}$ (C) 0 (D) $\frac{1}{2}$ (E) 1 (F) 2

8. (*1 point*)   Consider the Sturm-Liouville problem $y'' + \lambda^2 y = 0$, $y(0) = 0$, $y'(4) = 0$. Which λ and y are the solutions? (In the following, A is an arbitrary coefficient, and $n = 0, 1, 2, \ldots$.)

(A) $y = A \sin \lambda x, \quad \lambda = \dfrac{2n+1}{8}\pi$

(B) $y = A \sin \lambda x, \quad \lambda = \dfrac{2n+1}{6}\pi$

(C) $y = A \sin \lambda x, \quad \lambda = \dfrac{2n+1}{4}\pi$

(D) $y = A \sin \lambda x, \quad \lambda = \dfrac{2n+1}{2}\pi$

(E) $y = A \sin \lambda x, \quad \lambda = \dfrac{n}{8}\pi$

(F) $y = A \sin \lambda x, \quad \lambda = \dfrac{n}{4}\pi$

9. (*1 point*)   Give the Fourier series for

$$f(x) = \begin{cases} -\pi, & -\pi < x < -\frac{\pi}{2} \\ 0, & -\frac{\pi}{2} \leq x \leq \frac{\pi}{2} \\ \pi, & \frac{\pi}{2} < x < \pi \end{cases}$$

Ⓐ $2\sin x - 2\sin 2x + \dfrac{2}{3}\sin 3x + \dfrac{2}{5}\sin 5x - \dfrac{2}{3}\sin 6x + \dfrac{2}{7}\sin 7x + \cdots$

Ⓑ $2\sin x + 2\sin 2x + \dfrac{2}{3}\sin 3x + \dfrac{2}{5}\sin 5x + \dfrac{2}{3}\sin 6x + \dfrac{2}{7}\sin 7x + \cdots$

Ⓒ $2\sin x + 2\sin 2x + \dfrac{2}{3}\sin 3x - \dfrac{2}{5}\sin 5x - \dfrac{2}{3}\sin 6x - \dfrac{2}{7}\sin 7x + \cdots$

Ⓓ $2\sin x - 2\sin 2x + \dfrac{2}{3}\sin 3x + \dfrac{1}{2}\sin 4x + \dfrac{2}{5}\sin 5x - \dfrac{2}{3}\sin 6x + \dfrac{2}{7}\sin 7x + \cdots$

Ⓔ $2\sin x - 2\sin 2x + \dfrac{2}{3}\sin 3x + \dfrac{1}{2}\sin 4x + \dfrac{2}{5}\sin 5x + \dfrac{2}{3}\sin 6x + \dfrac{2}{7}\sin 7x + \cdots$

Ⓕ $2\sin x - 2\sin 2x + \dfrac{2}{3}\sin 3x + \dfrac{1}{2}\sin 4x - \dfrac{2}{5}\sin 5x - \dfrac{2}{3}\sin 6x + \dfrac{2}{7}\sin 7x + \cdots$

10. (*1 point*)   Consider the wave equation $u_{xx} = u_{tt}$ with boundary condition $u(0,t) = u(\pi, t) = 0$ for $t > 0$ and initial conditions $u(x,0) = \sin x$ and $u_t(x,0) = \cos x$. Let $U(x,s) = \mathcal{L}\{u(x,t)\}$ be the Laplace transform (in t). Give the ordinary differential equation satisfied by U (in x).

(A) $\dfrac{d^2U}{dx^2} - s^2U = s\sin x + \cos x$

(B) $\dfrac{d^2U}{dx^2} - s^2U = s\sin x - \cos x$

(C) $\dfrac{d^2U}{dx^2} - s^2U = -s\sin x - \cos x$

(D) $\dfrac{d^2U}{dx^2} - s^2U = \sin x + s\cos x$

(E) $\dfrac{d^2U}{dx^2} - s^2U = \sin x - s\cos x$

(F) $\dfrac{d^2U}{dx^2} - s^2U = -\sin x - s\cos x$

11. (*1 point*)   Give a harmonic conjugate for $u = \cos x \sinh y$.

(A) $\cos x \cosh y$ (B) $\cos y \sinh x$ (C) $-\cos x \sinh y$

(D) $\sin x \cosh y$ (E) $\sin x \sinh y$ (F) $-\sin x \cosh y$

12. (*1 point*)   Find k such that $x^5 - 10x^3y^2 + kxy^4 + i(5x^4y - 10x^2y^3 + y^5)$ is analytic.

(A) 1   (B) 2   (C) 3   (D) 4   (E) 5   (F) There is no such k.

13. (*1 point*)   Give a value of $i^{i/\pi}$.

(A) $e^{-1/2}$

(B) $e^{-1/2}(\cos\sqrt{2} + i\sin\sqrt{2})$

(C) $e^{-1} + e^{-1}i$

(D) $e^{-\pi^2/2}$

(E) $e^{-1}(\cos 1 + i\sin 1)$

(F) $e^{-2}(\cos 1 + i\sin 1)$

14. (*1 point*)   Consider a semicircle whose diameter is maintained at temperature 0 and whose circular edge is maintained at the temperature $u(1, \theta) = \sin 2\theta - \sin 3\theta$.

The steady-state temperature $u = u(r, \theta)$ satisfies $u_{rr} + \frac{1}{r} u_r + \frac{1}{r^2} u_{\theta\theta} = 0$. It is given by which of the following?

(A) $J_0(2r) \sin 2\theta - J_0(3r) \sin 3\theta$ (B) $\dfrac{J_0(2r)}{J_0(2)} \sin 2\theta - \dfrac{J_0(3r)}{J_0(3)} \sin 3\theta$

(C) $\dfrac{J_0(2r)}{2} \sin 2\theta - \dfrac{J_0(3r)}{3} \sin 3\theta$ (D) $\dfrac{J_0(2r)}{4} \sin 2\theta - \dfrac{J_0(3r)}{9} \sin 3\theta$

(E) $r^2 \sin 2\theta - r^3 \sin 3\theta$ (F) $r^4 \sin 2\theta - r^6 \sin 3\theta$

15. (*1 point*)   Evaluate

$$\oint_{|z|=1} e^{-\frac{1}{z}} \sin\frac{1}{z}\, dz .$$

(A) $-2\pi i$ (B) $-\pi i$ (C) 0 (D) πi (E) $2\pi i$ (F) $3\pi i$

16. (*1 point*) Evaluate

$$\int_{-\infty}^{\infty} \frac{dx}{(x^2+1)(x^2+4)}.$$

(A) $\frac{\pi}{6}$ (B) $\frac{\pi}{3}$ (C) $\frac{2\pi}{5}$ (D) $\frac{\pi}{2}$ (E) $\frac{\pi}{12}$ (F) $\frac{5\pi}{18}$

17.   (*1 point*)   Solve

$$u_{rr} + \frac{2}{r}u_r + \frac{1}{r^2}u_{\theta\theta} + \frac{\cot\theta}{r^2}u_\theta = 0$$

subject to the boundary condition $u(1,\theta) = \cos^3\theta$ for $0 < \theta < \pi$, and which is bounded at $r = 0$.

Recall that $\sin\theta\,\Theta'' + \cos\theta\,\Theta' + \lambda\sin\theta\,\Theta = 0$ has a solution $\Theta = P_n(\cos\theta)$ when $\lambda = n(n+1)$, where $P_n(x)$ is the nth Legendre polynomial.

The first four Legendre polynomials are $P_0(x) = 1$, $P_1(x) = x$, $P_2(x) = \frac{1}{2}(3x^2 - 1)$, and $P_3(x) = \frac{1}{2}(5x^3 - 3x)$.

(A) $\frac{3}{5}rP_1(\cos\theta) - \frac{2}{5}r^3P_3(\cos\theta)$ (B) $\frac{3}{5}rP_1(\cos\theta) + \frac{2}{5}r^3P_3(\cos\theta)$

(C) $\frac{1}{5}rP_1(\cos\theta) - \frac{3}{5}r^3P_3(\cos\theta)$ (D) $\frac{1}{5}rP_1(\cos\theta) + \frac{3}{5}r^3P_3(\cos\theta)$

(E) $\frac{3}{5}rP_1(\cos\theta) - \frac{1}{5}r^3P_3(\cos\theta)$ (F) $\frac{3}{5}rP_1(\cos\theta) + \frac{1}{5}r^3P_3(\cos\theta)$

18. (*1 point*)   The ordinary differential equation

$$3x^2y'' + (14x + x^2)y' - 4y = 0$$

has a general solution near $x = 0$ of the form $y = c_1 F(x) + c_2 \sqrt[3]{x}\,G(x)$, where $F(x)$ has a pole at 0 and $G(x)$ is analytic. What is the order of the pole of F at 0?

(A) 1   (B) 2   (C) 3   (D) 4   (E) 5   (F) 6

1. Find the radius of convergence for the Taylor series of $f(z) = \dfrac{1}{z^8 - 1}$

about the point $z = 2\sqrt{2} + 2\sqrt{2}i$.

(A) 1   (C) 2   (E) 3   (G) 4

(B) $\dfrac{3}{2}$ (D) $\dfrac{5}{2}$ (F) $\dfrac{7}{2}$ (H) ∞

---

2. Consider the Laurent series for the function

$$f(z) = \frac{z^2 - 2z + 3}{z - 2}$$

in the region $|z - 1| > 1$. What is the coefficient of the $(z-1)^{-2}$ term?

(A) -6 (C) -3 (E) 1   (G) 3

(B) -4 (D) 0   (F) 2   (H) 6

---

3. Find the constant k such that the function $v(x, y) = 3x^2 y + ky^3 - x + 1$ is a harmonic conjugate of the function $u(x, y) = x^3 - 3xy^2 + y$.

(A) -3 (C) -1 (E) 1   (G) 3

(B) -2 (D) 0   (F) 2   (H) 4

---

4. Evaluate

$$\int_0^{2i} e^{iz}\, dz.$$

(A) $i\left(1 - e^{-2}\right)$ (C) $1 - ie^{-2}$ (E) $i - e^{-2}$ (G) $1 - e^{-2}$

(B) $i\left(1 + e^{-2}\right)$ (D) $1 + ie^{-2}$ (F) $i + e^{-2}$ (H) $1 + e^{-2}$

5. Evaluate

$$\frac{i}{2}\oint_{|z|=1}\frac{\left(z^2-1\right)^2}{z^2\left(z+\frac{1}{2}\right)(z+2)}\,dz$$

(A) $\dfrac{\pi}{10}$

(B) $\dfrac{\pi}{8}$

(C) $\dfrac{\pi}{6}$

(D) $\dfrac{\pi}{4}$

(E) $\dfrac{\pi}{3}$

(F) $\dfrac{\pi}{2}$

(G) 1

(H) π

6. Evaluate

$$\int_0^{2\pi}\frac{d\theta}{2-\cos\theta}.$$

(A) π

(B) $\dfrac{2\pi}{\sqrt{3}}$

(C) $\dfrac{2\pi}{3}$

(D) $\dfrac{\pi}{2}$

(E) $\dfrac{\pi}{\sqrt{3}}$

(F) $\dfrac{\pi}{3}$

(G) $\dfrac{\pi}{4}$

(H) $\dfrac{\pi}{6}$

7. Evaluate

$$\int_{-\infty}^{\infty}\frac{dx}{x^2-6x+13}.$$

(A) $-\pi$

(B) $-\dfrac{\pi}{12}$

(C) $-\dfrac{\pi}{24}$

(D) 0

(E) $\dfrac{\pi}{24}$

(F) $\dfrac{\pi}{12}$

(G) $\dfrac{\pi}{2}$

(H) π

8. In the Fourier series expansion of $f(x) = 2x^2 - 1$ on $(-1,1)$ find the coefficient on the $\cos(4\pi x)$ term.

(A) 0 (C) $\dfrac{1}{2\pi}$ (E) $\dfrac{1}{2}$ (G) 1

(B) $\dfrac{1}{2\pi^2}$ (D) $\dfrac{2}{\pi^2}$ (F) $\dfrac{2}{\pi}$ (H) 2

9. Consider the Sturm-Liouville problem defined on $0 \le x \le \dfrac{\pi}{2}$:

$$y'' + \lambda y = 0 \qquad y(0) = 0, \ y'\left(\frac{\pi}{2}\right) = 0 \ .$$

Find all eigenvalues λ_n, $n = 0,1,2,\ldots$.

(A) $\lambda_n = n^2$ (C) $\lambda_n = \dfrac{n}{4}$ (E) $\lambda_n = \dfrac{(2n-1)\pi}{4}$ (G) $\lambda_n = \dfrac{(2n-1)^2\pi}{2}$

(B) $\lambda_n = \dfrac{n^2}{4}$ (D) $\lambda_n = \dfrac{(2n-1)\pi}{2}$ (F) $\lambda_n = (2n-1)^2$ (H) $\lambda_n = \dfrac{(2n-1)^2\pi}{4}$

10. The solution $u(x,t)$ defined for $0 \le x \le 2, t \ge 0$ to the wave equation

$$u_{tt} = u_{xx} \text{ with boundary conditions } u_x(0,t) = u_x(2,t) = 0 \text{ is}$$

$$u(x,t) = \sum_{n=0}^{\infty}\left[A_n \cos\left(\tfrac{n\pi}{2}t\right) + B_n \sin\left(\tfrac{n\pi}{2}t\right)\right]\cos\left(\tfrac{n\pi}{2}x\right).$$

Find $u\left(\dfrac{1}{3}, \dfrac{1}{2}\right)$ with initial conditions $u(x,0) = 3\cos(\pi x)$ and $u_t(x,0) = 2\cos(3\pi x)$.

(A) $\dfrac{1}{\pi}$ (C) $\dfrac{3}{\pi}$ (E) $\dfrac{2}{3\pi}$ (G) $\dfrac{1}{2}$

(B) $\dfrac{2}{\pi}$ (D) $\dfrac{1}{3\pi}$ (F) $\dfrac{1}{3}$ (H) 2

11. Let $u(x,t)$ be a function defined for $0 \le x \le \pi, t \ge 0$ such that

$$u_t = u_{xx} + 2u_x$$

with boundary conditions $u(0,t) = u(\pi,t) = 0$ for all $t \ge 0$

and initial condition $u(x,0) = e^{-x} \sin(2x)$.

Use separation of variables to find $u\left(\frac{\pi}{4}, 1\right)$.

(With separation constant $-\lambda$, you will find non-trivial solutions when $\lambda > 1$, say $\lambda = 1 + \alpha^2$)

(A) $e^{-1-\frac{\pi}{2}}$ (C) $e^{-5-\frac{\pi}{2}}$ (E) $e^{-1-\frac{\pi}{4}}$ (G) $e^{-5-\frac{\pi}{4}}$

(B) $e^{-2-\frac{\pi}{2}}$ (D) $e^{-10-\frac{\pi}{2}}$ (F) $e^{-2-\frac{\pi}{4}}$ (H) $e^{-10-\frac{\pi}{4}}$

12. Consider a circular plate of radius 1 whose circular edge is maintained at the temperature

$u(1,\theta) = \theta$. The steady-state temperature $u(r,\theta) = A_0 + \sum_{n=1}^{\infty} r^n \left[A_n \cos(n\theta) + B_n \sin(n\theta) \right]$

satisfies $u_{rr} + \frac{1}{r} u_r + \frac{1}{r^2} u_{\theta\theta} = 0$. Find the coefficient of the $\sin(3\theta)$ term.

(A) 0 (C) $\dfrac{2}{3}$ (E) $\dfrac{\pi}{3}$ (G) $\dfrac{2\pi}{3}$

(B) $\dfrac{1}{3}$ (D) $\dfrac{-2}{3}$ (F) $\dfrac{-\pi}{3}$ (H) $\dfrac{-2\pi}{3}$

SOLUTIONS:
1. E
2. G
3. C
4. A
5. H
6. B
7. G
8. B
9. F
10. E
11. G
12. D

Instructors D. Krashen and P. Storm   December 12, 2007

Math 241
Final examination

Instructions. Answer the following problems carefully and completely. Show all your work. Do not use a calculator. You may use both sides of one $8\frac{1}{2} \times 11$ sheet of paper for handwritten notes you wrote yourself. Please turn in your sheet of notes with your exam. There are 100 points possible. Good luck!

Name _____ Solutions _____

Instructors's name _____

TA's name and time _____

1.	(2)	_____
2.	(14)	_____
3.	(6)	_____
4.	(2)	_____
5.	(3)	_____
6.	(8)	_____
7.	(8)	_____
8.	(5)	_____
9.	(5)	_____
10.	(10)	_____
11.	(11)	_____
12.	(6)	_____
13.	(6)	_____
14.	(14)	_____
Total (100)		_____

1

Here are some integrals you can use:

$$\int_0^\infty xe^{-x} \sin(cx)\, dx = \frac{2c}{(1+c^2)^2}$$

$$\int_0^\infty xe^{-x} \cos(cx)\, dx = \frac{1-c^2}{(1+c^2)^2}$$

1. Write whether the following statement is true or false. (You do not need to show any work.) The product of an odd function f with an odd function g is an odd function.

FALSE

2. Use a Fourier transform, a sine transform, or a cosine transform to find the displacement $u(x,t)$, for $x > 0$ and $t > 0$, of a semi-infinite string if

$$u(0,t) = 0, \quad u(x,0) = xe^{-x}, \quad \text{and} \quad \left.\frac{\partial u}{\partial t}\right|_{t=0} = 0.$$

You may assume the constant a^2 of the wave equation is equal to 1. Your final answer may contain an integral.

Let $\quad U(\alpha, t) = \int_0^\infty u(x,t) \sin(\alpha x)\, dx \quad$ be the

sign transform of $u(x,t)$.

$\mathcal{F}_S\left\{\dfrac{\partial^2 u}{\partial x^2}\right\} = -\alpha^2\, U(\alpha, t) + \alpha\, u(0, t)$

$\qquad\qquad = -\alpha^2\, U(\alpha, t)$

$\mathcal{F}_S\left\{\dfrac{\partial^2 u}{\partial t^2}\right\} = \dfrac{\partial^2 U}{\partial t^2}.$

$\therefore$ the wave eqn $\quad \dfrac{\partial^2 u}{\partial x^2} = \dfrac{\partial^2 u}{\partial t^2} \quad$ transforms to

$\qquad -\alpha^2 U(\alpha, t) = \dfrac{\partial^2 U}{\partial t^2}.$

$\Rightarrow \quad U(\alpha, t) = A\cos(\alpha t) + B\sin(\alpha t)$

$\qquad$ where A & B are fcts of α alone.

$0 = \mathcal{F}_S\{0\} = \mathcal{F}_S\left\{\left.\dfrac{\partial u}{\partial t}\right|_{t=0}\right\} = \left.\dfrac{\partial U}{\partial t}\right|_{t=0}$

3

$$\Rightarrow \quad B = 0 \quad \Rightarrow \quad \bar{U}(\alpha, t) = A \cos(\alpha t).$$

$$A = \bar{U}(\alpha, 0) = \widetilde{\mathcal{F}}_S\{u(x,0)\} = \widetilde{\mathcal{F}}_S\{x e^{-x}\} = \frac{2\alpha}{(1+\alpha^2)^2}.$$

$$\Rightarrow \quad \bar{U}(\alpha, t) = \frac{2\alpha}{(1+\alpha^2)^2} \cdot \cos(\alpha t).$$

$$\Rightarrow \quad u(x,t) = \widetilde{\mathcal{F}}_S^{-1}\{\bar{U}(\alpha, t)\} = \frac{2}{\pi} \int_0^\infty \frac{2\alpha}{(1+\alpha^2)^2} \cos(\alpha t) \sin(\alpha x)\, d\alpha$$

3. Find *any two* independent solutions $u(x, y)$ to the following PDE:

$$\frac{\partial^2 u}{\partial x \partial y} = u$$

Neither of your solutions can be the zero function.

e^{x+y} is one solution.

$e^{2x + 1/2}$ is another solution.

$$\frac{e^{x+y}}{e^{2x+1/2}} = e^{-x + 1/2} \quad \text{is not a constant fct}$$

$$\Rightarrow \text{ they are independent.}$$

4. Find a and b real numbers such that

$$\frac{10 - 5i}{6 + 2i} = a + ib.$$

$$\frac{(10 - 5i)(6 - 2i)}{36 + 4} = \frac{60 - 30i - 20i - 10}{40}$$

$$= \frac{5}{4} - \frac{5}{4} i$$

$$\Rightarrow \quad a = \frac{5}{4}, \quad b = -\frac{5}{4}.$$

5. Let

$$z_1 = 2\cos(\pi/8) + 2i\sin(\pi/8)$$
$$z_2 = 4\cos(3\pi/8) + 4i\sin(3\pi/8)$$

Find a and b real numbers such that

$$\frac{z_1}{z_2} = a + ib.$$

$$z_1 = 2e^{\pi i/8} \qquad z_2 = 4e^{3\pi i/8}$$

$$\frac{z_1}{z_2} = \frac{2e^{\pi i/8}}{4e^{3\pi i/8}} = \frac{1}{2}e^{-\frac{2\pi i}{8}} = \frac{1}{2}e^{-\frac{\pi i}{4}} = \frac{1}{2}\left(\frac{1}{\sqrt{2}} - \frac{i}{\sqrt{2}}\right)$$

$$a = \frac{1}{2\sqrt{2}} \qquad b = \frac{-1}{2\sqrt{2}}$$

6. Show the complex function $f(z) = \bar{z}$ is not analytic at $z = 0$.

I will show the limit $\lim\limits_{z \to 0} \dfrac{f(z) - f(0)}{\bar{z}} = \lim\limits_{z \to 0} \dfrac{\bar{z}}{z}$ does not exist.

First let $z = x$ for x real.

$$\lim\limits_{z \to 0} \frac{\bar{z}}{z} = \lim\limits_{x \to 0} \frac{\bar{x}}{x} = \lim\limits_{x \to 0} \frac{x}{x} = 1.$$

Now let $z = iy$ for y real.

$$\lim\limits_{z \to 0} \frac{\bar{z}}{z} = \lim\limits_{y \to 0} \frac{\overline{iy}}{iy} = \lim\limits_{y \to 0} \frac{-iy}{iy} = -1.$$

This shows the limit does not exist.

7. Find all points z in $\mathbb{C}$ satisfying the equation

$$\sin z = 2.$$

Write the solutions in the form $a + ib$ for a and b real numbers.

$$2 = \sin z = \frac{1}{2i}\left(e^{iz} - e^{-iz}\right)$$

$$4i\, e^{iz} = \left(e^{iz}\right)^2 - 1$$

$$\left(e^{iz}\right)^2 - 4i\, e^{iz} - 1 = 0.$$

$$e^{iz} = \frac{4i + (-16+4)^{1/2}}{2} = 2i \pm \frac{1}{2}i\sqrt{12}$$

$$= 2i \pm i\sqrt{3} = i\left(2 \pm \sqrt{3}\right).$$

Let $z = x + iy$. Then

$$e^{iz} = e^{-y}e^{ix} = i\left(2 \pm \sqrt{3}\right)$$

For $i(2+\sqrt{3})$
$$\begin{cases} 2+\sqrt{3} > 0 \;\Rightarrow\; \arg(i(2+\sqrt{3})) = \frac{\pi}{2} \;\Rightarrow\; x = \frac{\pi}{2} + 2\pi n. \\[2mm] |e^{iz}| = |e^{-y}| = e^{-y} = |i(2+\sqrt{3})| = 2+\sqrt{3}. \;\Rightarrow\; y = -\log(2 \\[2mm] \text{So one set of sol'ns is } \frac{\pi}{2} + 2\pi n - i\log(2+\sqrt{3}) \\[2mm] \text{for } n \text{ any integer.} \end{cases}$$

For $i(2-\sqrt{3})$
$$\begin{cases} \text{Similarly } 2-\sqrt{3} > 0 \;\Rightarrow\; \text{the other set of sol'ns} \\[2mm] \text{is } \frac{\pi}{2} + 2\pi n - i\log(2-\sqrt{3}) \text{ for } n \text{ any integer.} \end{cases}$$

8

8. Compute the contour integral

$$\oint_C \frac{z}{z^2 - \pi^2}\, dz$$

where C is the circle $|z| = 3$.

The fct. $\frac{z}{z^2-\pi^2}$ ~~has~~ is not analytic at $\pm\pi$

Neither of these points lie inside C.

$\therefore$ by Cauchy's thm

$$\oint_C \frac{z}{z^2-\pi^2}\, dz = 0.$$

9

9. Determine the pole(s) of $5 - 6/z^2$. Find the order(s) of the pole(s). Compute the residue(s) at the pole(s).

The fct. $f(z) = 5 - 6/z^2$ is already written in the form of a Laurent series centered at 0, where it has a pole of order 2 with residue 0.

$f(z)$ has no other poles.

10. Determine the pole(s) of

$$\frac{1}{1 - e^z}.$$

Find the order(s) of the pole(s). Compute the residue(s) at the pole(s).

Let $f(z) = \frac{1}{1-e^z}$. $f(z)$ is $2\pi i$-periodic, i.e. $f(z + 2\pi i) = f(z)$.

$f(z)$ is not analytic at $z = 0$. Let's examine this singularity first

Consider $g(z) = \dfrac{e^z - 1}{z} = 1 + \dfrac{z}{2!} + \dfrac{z^2}{3!} + \dfrac{z^3}{4!} + \cdots$

By the ratio test this power series converges on all of $\mathbb{C}$.

$\Rightarrow$ $g(z)$ is analytic everywhere. $g(0) = 1$.

$\Rightarrow$ $\dfrac{d}{dz}\left(\dfrac{z}{1-e^z}\right) = \dfrac{d}{dz}\left(\dfrac{-1}{g(z)}\right) = -1 \cdot (-1) \cdot (g(z))^{-2} \cdot g'(z)$

$\Rightarrow$ $\dfrac{d}{dz}\Big|_{z=0}\left(\dfrac{z}{1-e^z}\right) = g'(0) = \dfrac{1}{2}$.

$\Rightarrow$ $\dfrac{z}{1-e^z}$ is analytic at 0. $\Rightarrow$ $f(z)$ has a simple pole at 0. The residue at 0 is

$\lim\limits_{z \to 0}\left(\dfrac{z}{1-e^z}\right) = -\dfrac{1}{\lim\limits_{z \to 0} g(z)} = -1$.

By the $2\pi i$-periodicity of $f(z)$, the other poles are at $2\pi i n$ for n any integer, and these poles are all simple with residue -1.

11. Compute the integral

$$\int_0^\pi \frac{1}{5 + 4\cos\theta}\, d\theta$$

$\cos\theta$ is even so

$$\int_0^\pi \frac{d\theta}{5+4\cos\theta} = \frac{1}{2}\int_{-\pi}^{\pi} \frac{d\theta}{5+4\cos\theta} = \frac{1}{2}\int_{-\pi}^{\pi} \frac{d\theta}{5+2e^{i\theta}+2e^{-i\theta}} = \frac{1}{2}\int \frac{1}{ie^{i\theta}} \frac{ie^{i\theta}\,d\theta}{5+2e^{i\theta}+2e^{-i\theta}}$$

Let $C(\theta) = e^{i\theta}$ for $-\pi \le \theta \le \pi$.

$$= \frac{1}{2i}\oint_C \frac{1}{z}\frac{dz}{5+2z+2/z} = \frac{1}{2i}\oint_C \frac{dz}{2z^2+5z+2} = \frac{1}{2i}\oint_C \frac{dz}{2(z+2)(z+\frac{1}{2})}$$

$$\frac{-5 \pm \sqrt{25-16}}{4} = \text{~~~~} = \left\{\frac{-8}{4}, \frac{-2}{4}\right\} = \left\{-2, -\tfrac{1}{2}\right\}$$

$$= \frac{1}{4i} \cdot 2\pi i \cdot \text{Res}\left(\frac{1}{(z+2)(z+\frac{1}{2})},\ -\tfrac{1}{2}\right)$$

only the simple pole $-\tfrac{1}{2}$ lies inside C

$$= \frac{\pi}{2}\ \frac{1}{(-\frac{1}{2}+2)} = \frac{\pi}{3}$$

12

12. Let C be the curve in the complex plane parametrized by $C'(t) = \cos(t) + i\sin(t)$. for $0 \leq t \leq \pi$. (Note the π!) Compute the value of the contour integral

$$\int_C \frac{dz}{z^2}$$

$C(t) = \cos t + i \sin t = e^{it} \qquad 0 \leq t \leq \pi$

$C'(t) = ie^{it}$

$$\int_C \frac{dz}{z^2} = \int_0^\pi \frac{1}{e^{2it}} \cdot ie^{it}\, dt = i \int_0^\pi e^{-it}\, dt$$

$$= \frac{i}{-i} \cdot \left[e^{-it} \right]_0^\pi = -1 \cdot (-1 - 1) = 2$$

14

13. Consider the function

$$f(x) = \begin{cases} 0 & \text{for } 0 \le x \le 1 \\ 1 & \text{for } 1 < x \le 2 \end{cases}$$

defined on the interval $[0, 2]$. Let

$$\sum_{n=1}^{\infty} B_n \sin\left(\frac{n\pi x}{2}\right)$$

be a sine series for $f(x)$. Using the same values for B_n, for all x in the real line
define a function

$$g(x) = \sum_{n=1}^{\infty} B_n \sin\left(\frac{n\pi x}{2}\right).$$

Find $g(-5/2)$ and $g(-5)$.

f has a jump discontinuity at 1

$g(x)$ is a 4π-periodic fct.

$\Rightarrow g\left(-\frac{5}{2}\right) = g\left(-\frac{5}{2} + \frac{8}{2}\right) = g\left(\frac{3}{2}\right) = f\left(\frac{3}{2}\right) = 1.$

$g(-5) = g(-1) = -g(1) = -f(1) = -\frac{1}{2}(0+1)$

g is odd

$= -\frac{1}{2}.$

15

14. Solve the Laplace equation $u_{xx} + u_{yy} = 0$ for a function $u(x,y)$ with $0 \le x \le 2$, $0 \le y \le 1$ and boundary conditions:

$$u(0,y) = 0, \quad \frac{\partial u}{\partial x}(2,y) = 0, \quad u(x,0) = 0,$$

$$u(x,1) = 3\sin\left(\frac{\pi x}{4}\right) - 2\sin\left(\frac{5\pi x}{4}\right).$$

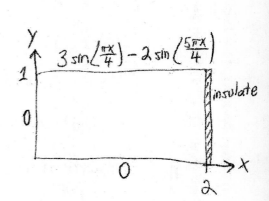

$u(x,y) = F(x) \cdot G(y)$

$F''(x)\, G(y) + F(x) \cdot G''(y) = 0$

$\Rightarrow \quad \dfrac{F''(x)}{F(x)} = -\dfrac{G''(y)}{G(y)} = -\lambda.$

$F''(x) + \lambda F(x) = 0 \qquad F(0) = F'(2) = 0$

$\lambda > 0$: Let $\alpha = \sqrt{+\lambda}$.

$F(x) = A\cos(\alpha x) + B\sin(\alpha x)$

$F(0) = 0 \Rightarrow A = 0$

$F'(x) = \alpha B \cos(\alpha \cdot 2) = 0 \qquad \Rightarrow \qquad 2\alpha = \frac{\pi}{2} + \pi n$

$\Rightarrow \quad \alpha = \frac{\pi}{4} + \frac{\pi}{2}n \quad \text{for} \quad n = 0, 1, 2, 3, \ldots$

$\lambda = 0$: $F(x) = Ax + B \qquad F(0) = 0 \Rightarrow B = 0$

$F'(2) = A = 0.$

So 0 is not an eigenvalue.

16

$\lambda < 0$

~~case~~ : $F(x) = A\cosh(\alpha x) + B\sinh(\alpha x)$ for $\alpha = \sqrt{\lambda}$.

$F(0) = 0 \Rightarrow A = 0$.

$F'(2) = B\alpha\cosh(2\alpha) = 0 \Rightarrow B = 0$.

$\Rightarrow$ no eigenvalues < 0.

So the eigenvalues ~~are~~ are $\lambda_n = \left(\frac{\pi}{4} + \frac{\pi n}{2}\right)^2$ for $n = 0,1,2,3,$

with eigen fct $F_n(x) = B_n \sin(\sqrt{+\lambda_n} \cdot x)$.

$\Rightarrow G_n''(y) = \lambda_n G_n(y)$ & $G_n(0) = 0$

$\Rightarrow G_n(y) = C_n \sinh(\sqrt{\lambda_n} \cdot y)$.

$\Rightarrow U_n(x,y) = A_n \sinh\left(\left(\frac{\pi}{4} + \frac{\pi n}{2}\right) y\right) \cdot \sin\left(\left(\frac{\pi}{4} + \frac{\pi n}{2}\right) x\right)$ for $n = 0,1,2,$

& $u(x,y) = \sum_{n=0}^{\infty} U_n(x,y)$.

$u(x,1) = 3\sin\left(\frac{\pi x}{4}\right) - 2\sin\left(\frac{5\pi x}{4}\right) = \sum_{n=0}^{\infty} A_n \sinh\left(\left(\frac{\pi}{4} + \frac{\pi n}{2}\right)\right) \sin\left(\left(\frac{\pi}{4} + \frac{\pi n}{2}\right)\right)$

$\Rightarrow$ only the $n=0$ and $n=2$ coeff. are nonzero

$A_0 = \frac{3}{\sinh\left(\frac{\pi}{4}\right)}$, $A_2 = \frac{-2}{\sinh\left(\frac{5\pi}{4}\right)}$

& $u(x,y) = \frac{3}{\sinh\left(\frac{\pi}{4}\right)} \cdot \sinh\left(\frac{\pi y}{4}\right) \sin\left(\frac{\pi x}{4}\right) - \frac{2}{\sinh\left(\frac{5\pi}{4}\right)} \cdot \sinh\left(\frac{5\pi y}{4}\right) \sin\left(\frac{5\pi x}{4}\right)$.

17